BUDDHISM

for Beginners

Modern guide on
Buddhist rituals, practices
and teachings

by

Dharma Hazari

Get the FREE Bonus NOW!

First and foremost, I'd like to congratulate you for purchasing this book. Curiosity is a diminishing trait nowadays. But you have chosen to open your mind to the new knowledge contained in this book. That's a great sign. As the ancient Chinese quote goes, *"When the student is ready, the teacher will appear."*

But first, I want you to understand that learning about things like Buddhism, spirituality, yoga, meditation etc. can sometimes be lonely and unfruitful without proper support. That is why I have created a set of PDF guides and a Facebook community that you can get for FREE. You can get access to these resources by signing up at the list below. It's an exclusive list and you only need to enter your e-mail ID to join. So that's a clear win-win. You can go ahead and sign up at the link below now.

www.bit.ly/dharma-hazari-subscribe

About the Author

Hello there! I am Dharma Hazari. I grew up in India which is a hotbed for all kinds of world religions. I have been practicing Buddhism, Yoga, Meditation for nearly 8 years now. Initially, I just took it up to see if I can improve my focus and concentration. With support from my guru, I was able to setup a daily practice and monitor my results. The progress was slow but steady. I experienced tremendous boost in my productivity, a great sense of inner well-being and empathy. The change was very much noticeable. All my friends and family would ask me what my secret sauce was.

Since then, I've been guiding other people in their own journey to eliminate inner conflicts.

I'm a student of Science and do not believe in baseless theories and misguided beliefs. This book is an honest attempt to convey my understanding of Buddhism and its core principles. A lot of time and effort have gone into preparing this book for you. I sincerely hope you can gain something valuable after finishing it. Good Luck!

If you are someone who is interested in such things as yoga, meditation and spirituality then I highly recommend you to join my list (link below). You will get to receive my latest books for FREE or at a heavily discounted price. You will also be part of a community of truth seekers and beautiful souls.

www.bit.ly/dharma-hazari

Why You Should Read This Book

Wisdom means learning from other's mistakes. Books are like distilled knowledge capsules that you can consume to make your reality a little bit brighter. I've noticed in my own life that great books have the power to clean the windows through which we look at the world.

This book in particular, has been designed to give you a concise understanding of what Buddhism entails and how one can gain benefits from its practices like Vipassana, Zen, Mindfulness etc. Among other things, you will learn why Buddhism is considered to be one of the most scientific religions currently in practice. And also, you'll get to understand the core philosophies, values and teachings of the Buddha that are essential for Buddhism. Without further ado, let's get started.

Table of Contents

Chatper-1: The Story of Siddhartha

Let us begin by learning the origin story of Buddhism. We will be looking briefly at the backstory of this incredible eastern religion and answering questions like "where was it founded?", "who founded it?", "how?", "when?" etc. You are advised to keep in mind that certain historical data presented here is prone to slight error since an accurate recording of the facts does not exist.

The religion of Buddhism gets its name from a man called as *The Buddha* whose original name was Siddhartha Gautama. The name

Siddhartha in Sanskrit language means *one who has attained his purpose*. And Gautama means one who dispels darkness through his brilliance. Siddartha was apparently given his second name of Gautama in appreciation of his foster mother Gautami. He was born around 563 B.C in a place called Lumbini in Nepal which is at the foot of the great Himalayan mountains.

His mother was Maya and his father was Suddhodana, a prominent leader of the Shakya clan. Some historians say that they were actually the King and Queen of the country. As per the Indian caste system, they were Kshatriyas (warrior tribe) ruling from the capital city of Kapilavasthu. Suddhodana had a second wife named Pajapati Gotami who was the sister of

Maya. They were both princesses from the Koliya clan.

Legend has it that one night of full moon, Maya had a vivid dream in which a white elephant holding a white lotus flower in its trunk appeared and went around her three times before entering her womb from the right side. Now, the elephant has very special consideration in both the Indian and Nepalese cultures. So, the couple called for sages and wise men to figure out what the dream signified. The wise men, after hearing Maya's dream predicted that their child will be a great leader unlike the world had ever seen.

10 months after the dream, Maya left for her parent's home since it was the tradition

at the time and still is in some parts of India) to leave the husband and stay with parents during a woman's pregnancy. On her way from Kapilavasthu, they encountered a beautiful park near Lumbini with lots of flowers and birds. The queen decided to hault at this park and rest under a sala tree when Siddhartha was born.

After the birth of Siddhartha, Maya returned to Kapilavasthu where Suddhodana and the people of the kingdom were ecstatic to hear the news of their prince's birth. However, seven days after the prince's birth, queen Maya died. That same day, her sister, Gotami gave birth to a boy named Nanda. It was Gotami who raised Siddhartha as her own son making sure he never felt the lack of a motherly presence. She would later become his first female disciple and follower of Buddhism.

Siddhartha grew up as a very kind, brave and intelligent man excelling in warrior sports like horse riding, archery as well as education. However, the king was afraid that his son might leave him to become an ascetic. And also, to shield Siddhartha from the ugliness and suffering outside the palace, he employed special guards and servants to make sure Siddhartha would never see or go beyond the palace walls. However, as time went on he noticed that the prince was starting to feel dissatisfied by the palace life. After heeding the sages' advice, he arranged for a gathering of the kingdom's most beautiful princesses for his son to pick from. Among them was

Yasodhara, daughter of Suppabuddha and Pamita was the sister of Suddhodana, Siddhartha's father. They also came from the same royal Shakya family which made Yasodhara Siddhartha's cousin. Seeing her charm, beauty and kindness, Siddhartha approached Yasodhara and gifted her the most valuable present he had with him at the moment. Thus, Siddhartha and Yasodhara were soon married in a grand ceremony, all set to become the future king and queen of Kapilavasthu.

Days passed by without much turbulence as Siddhartha and Yasodhara rejoiced their early days of marriage. However, a curiosity for seeing what lies beyond the walls took over Siddhartha as he was not happy living like a prisoner inside the palace. One day he asked his father about it and the king arranged for a grand visit of his son, the noble prince, around the city. Decorations were made throughout the kingdom and people dressed up to welcome their prince. So, Siddhartha went with his charioteer Channa to see his city. Although everything looked good from the outside, he noticed a frail old man on the streets. He was bent over with weakness, had no teeth and relied on a stick to support his weight. Seeing this, Siddhartha was confused and taken aback. "Who is that Channa? And why is he in such suffering?" Siddhartha asked his charioteer. "He is an old beggar, my prince. When he was young, he was strong but with old age comes weakness and suffering." Siddhartha, feeling a bit sad but still curious, asked "Is this how I shall become, as time passes? Is this what awaits all of us?". To this Channa replied, "Yes my prince. Ageing is a law of nature. Everyone, if they are able to live long enough, shall become old and frail like this beggar. It cannot be stopped." These words struck deep into siddhartha's mind and heart for he had never witnessed old age or death inside the palace.

After coming back to the palace from his visit, Siddhartha did not speak to anyone for a while. He was pondering over what he had just experienced. A terrible fate awaited him and all his beloved. And he could do nothing to stop it. After hearing what had happened, the king Suddhodana felt worried for his son. So, he ordered for more dances, drinks and celebration to distract Siddhartha from this unfortunate reality. However, Siddhartha wanted to resolve the conflict that arose in him. He asked the king to arrange for a secret tour of the city where he would go in disguise and observe the people and their lives. The king saw that there was no denying siddhartha. So, he complied with the request although unwillingly.

Thus, it happened that Siddhartha again found himself in disguise as a nobleman, observing his city and its people. It looked very different this time around. There were no more decorations and celebrations. People were busy with their day-to-day activities and they seemed content. However, as they walked more, Siddhartha saw a man lying on the ground, his hands clenched over his stomach. The man was crying and in severe pain. He had purple patches all over his body. Siddhartha rant to the man and helped him rest his head on Siddhartha's knee. Seeing as he was in severe pain and could not talk but only cry, Siddhartha asked "What is wrong with this man, Channa?". "He is sick, my prince. He has a rare plague disease which has poisoned his blood. I pray you don't touch him lest it spread to you as well." To this, Siddhartha asked, "Are there more people like this, Channa? Can't this be stopped?". Channa responded, "Yes, my prince. There are many more people suffering with different kinds of diseases in the world. It may happen to anyone and there is no way to stop it."

Hearing this made Siddhartha sad for it felt like pain was not only widespread in the world but also inevitable in many circumstances. He came back to the palace and yet again went into a deep contemplative state. After a few weeks, he was ready for another trip to the city. So, he got dressed as a nobleman again and went with Channa out of the palace. After walking for a while, they came across a procession of people. At the center of the crows were four men carrying a big plank of wood on which a man was lying with eyes closed and without any movement. Siddhartha and Channa followed the procession which ended with the motionless man on the plank being put on a big pile of wood that was soon set on fire. The man lay there without making any noise or movement. Siddhartha had never seen anything like this before in his life. "Why is the man letting himself be lit on fire,

Channa?" he asked. "The man is dead, my prince." Channa replied. "Dead! What does that mean?" Siddhartha asked with honest curiosity. "Death is the ending of all life, my prince. It is a law of nature. Everyone who is born must die one day."

What a terrible tragedy life is, Siddhartha thought. It all seemed like a beautiful never-ending story just a while back. But now he felt distanced from his happiness. The idea of old age, suffering and death brought gloom in his heart. Yet there was a deep longing in him to reach nirvana and experience ever-lasting happiness and inner peace. He set forth again after a few days from the palace to visit the city. This time, he noticed a man in orange robes with all his hair shaved off. "Who is this man,

Channa? And why does he look so happy?" Siddhartha asked. "He is a sadhu(monk), my prince. He has given up all that is his and now travels from house to house offering his wisdom and receiving food from people." The prince was amused and also excited to hear this. Somehow, he felt associated with that kind of lifestyle. He continued his journey until his legs were tired and then sat under a tree to rest. After a while, a messenger came to announce that the prince had become a father. His wife, the princess Yasodhara had given birth to a beautiful young boy. However, Siddhartha felt that the boy was yet another attachment, trying to stop him from pursuing his path. Thus, the boy was named "Rahula" which in Sanksrit translates to "obstruction" or hindrance.

The next day, a grand feast was thrown in the name of the new born heir to the throne. All the best dancers, singers and cooks were invited to perform in the palace for the celebrations. Yet Siddhartha's mind wasn't present in the moment. He always seemed distracted and sad. That night, while the whole city of Kapilavasthu was asleep, Siddhartha went to his wife's chambers quietly and saw his son for the first time. He took leave of his sleeping wife and son, vowing to himself that he would return once he found what he was looking for. Then, he went and woke Channa up who saddled his horse. Silently they left the palace and the whole city and reached a river bank. There, Siddhartha cut his hair off, removed all his jewelry and fancy clothing until he was left with nothing but a simple robe and an empty bowl. He would go live the life of a monk, leaving all his family behind, in search of the solution. He gave Channa all his ornaments and sent him back with the horse. His journey had just begun.

As he travelled in his new avatar, people started to call him Shakyamuni or "Sage of Shakyas" for he was wise, polite, clean and nothing like a beggar. People were more than happy to give him food. After a while, Siddhartha found a guru known as Alara Kalama who was popular at that time in India, for teaching meditation. So, Siddhartha studied under him and soon enough acquired knowledge and skill that equaled his guru. Although Alara Kalama asked him to stay, he left in search of an answer and eventually found another guru named Uddaka. He studied under him as well but soon realized that none of the gurus were helping him find a solution to suffering. Thus, Siddhartha finally set out on his own to figure it out himself.

He went to a place called Uruvela where he made 5 friends who also had left their palaces to pursue a life of spirituality as ascetics. Siddhartha spent six years in Uruvela trying all sorts of stuff to attain wisdom. He practiced extreme fasting eating only one grain of rice per day. All the flesh and color left his body and he appeared to be a living skeleton. He would follow the path of austerity in arriving at the answer. No food, no water and often no breath as well. Just meditation. While he was extremely close to death in his pursuit of enlightenment, a girl saw him and the 5 ascetics. She got curious and came closer to see that Siddhartha was meditating with eyes closed but he looked extremely sick and weak. So, she offered him sustenance which he consumed. Seeing as it brought back energy to his body, Siddhartha realized that torturing the body is no way to attain enlightenment. "I shall follow the middle path.", he said. The five friends felt that Siddhartha lost command over himself and that he did not take the path to enlightenment seriously enough. So, they abandoned him. But Siddhartha continued his life and pursuit.

One evening on the eve of the full moon, Siddhartha sat under a banyan tree in a village called Gaya. He resolved to not move from that spot until he had attained the highest of wisdom and enlightenment to end all human suffering. As he meditated intensely, thoughts of evil nature (symbolically referred to as the evil god Mara and his army) crept up into his mind. But Siddhartha rose above them all and did not fall for desire, fear, craving or attachment. He felt peaceful as he let all those thoughts come and go. As night came, he could see segments from his past lives. And even further into the night, he saw how all life was temporary and the true nature of birth, death and rebirth. Deeper into the night, he realized the cause of all suffering and how to attain vimukthi (freedom) from it.

All the stories and the legends say that at this point of liberation, Siddhartha was no longer Siddhartha. He became The Buddha or The Enlightened One. He could see reality for what it is, without any desire. This was Dharma or how things are in reality. He was able to see his past lives and all their deeds. He saw karma in effect i.e., how humans were being born and dead in cycles. It didn't matter if they did good or bad deeds. They were all a part of this cycle. But this was it for him. His cycle had come to an end. He had no more rebirth. All desires, illusions and ignorance left him. He was now truly enlightened.

The banyan tree in Sanskrit is known as "Bodhi" tree. Some say that that's how the

Buddha got his name – because he got enlightened under a Bodhi tree.

The legend says that the Buddha spent a few weeks under the Bodhi tree after enlightenment, rejoicing the utter bliss of existence. But after a while, he heard the voice of Lord Brahma, the creator, who asked him to spread his wisdom and learning among fellow humans. So, the Buddha started travelling and spreading his knowledge on how to live life without suffering. In the next chapter, we will be looking at his teachings in detail.

Chatper-2: The Four Noble Truths

The Four Noble Truths are what The Buddha taught his early disciples and other eventual followers. They are seen as the guiding pathway to enlightenment. The spiritual dimension is like a maze. You can get lost easily if you follow the wrong guru or take the wrong steps. Just as early mountain climbers set up trail for subsequent climbers, so too has the Buddha laid out a framework for achieving enlightenment. Realizing that many people will come to see the four noble truths as doctrines, the Buddha said, "Think of it as a finger pointing to the moon. Anyone who focuses on the finger itself will miss out on the moon." This particular anecdote has inspired the famous dialogue of Bruce Lee in the movie "Enter the Dragon".

All those who seek enlightenment in Buddhism are expected to fully understand and accept these four noble truths. And those that do are presumed to have acquired the eyes to perceive enlightenment.

Noble Truth #1: Dukkha (Suffering)

Birth is suffering, Ageing is suffering, Illness is suffering, Death is suffering, Union with what is displeasing is suffering, Separation from what is pleasing is suffering, Unfulfilled desire is suffering. In essence, life that is not free from desire and passion will have some element of suffering in it.

Noble Truth #2: Samudaya (Cause of Suffering)

The cause of all suffering is "tanha" which means greed or desire. It is this that makes our physical body crave for sensual pleasure and enslaves us to the natural instincts. This happens even when what we desire is not exactly beneficial to us. That is the nature of desire – to enslave.

Noble Truth #3: Nirodha (End of Suffering)

The Buddha states that the end of Dukkha or suffering is to let go of painful attachments. This means that there will no longer be a constant craving for material or spiritual things. Freedom from suffering can be attained when the compulsive pursuit of pleasure comes to a halt.

Noble Truth #4: Marga (Path to end Suffering)

This is the noble truth that The Buddha had spent most of his time preaching because it holds the solution to all human suffering. And according to this, there are eight areas of self-development that are necessary to walk the path of enlightenment. Also called "The Eightfold Path", these practices touch every part of our life and help us rearrange ourselves in such a way that there is least resistance with the force of life.

The Eightfold Path

In many Buddhist artifacts, drawings the eightfold path is represented as a "dharma wheel" (dharmachakra) consisting of eight spokes that represent the eight different aspects of this path. So, they're all linked together and aid in the complete development of body, mind and spirit. However, anyone who decides to follow the eightfold path totally and in harmony with the Buddhist truths and values is expected to possess a high amount of discipline. Liberation from suffering doesn't come cheap. Only one who is unwavering in their pursuit will reach the goal.

But luckily, the eight folds of the path are interconnected. So, walking on one will build you up to walk on others as well. And also, it's not suggested that you approach them sequentially like an assignment. Rather, you should adapt a well-rounded approach and develop all the virtues simultaneously. All of this is specifically geared towards the individual's attainment of nirvana or a state of enlightenment. Let us look at them in further detail.

1. Right Understanding (Samyag Dhrishti)
2. Right Intent (Samyak Sankalpa)
3. Right Speech (Samyag Vac)
4. Right Action (Samyak Karmanta)
5. Right Livelihood (Samyag Ajiva)
6. Right Effort (Samyag Vyayama)
7. Right Mindfulness (Samyak Smriti)
8. Right Concentration (Samyag Samadhi)

Right Understanding

Right understanding or Right View is an important step in the eightfold path. It says that we need to look at reality for what it is and not what we want it to be. With the right perspective, we can stop letting our personal inflictions effect reality or our idea of it. Right understanding is like knowing how to read the map. Without it, you cannot navigate through life. However, we must keep in mind that reading the map is not the same as walking through it. Personal experience is the only way to true understanding.

Right Intent

This is another crucial element of the noble path. Without the right intent, your direction in life will sway towards the sub-optimal and that cannot lead you to enlightenment. You need to look deep within yourself and understand what your heart wants. Out of this will come the right intent. Consider this example. Suppose you're a mountain climber and you have acquired the right understanding of the climbing techniques and the landscape. Without a strong intention of getting to the top, will you be able to endure the hardship? In this example, the mountain refers to life, the top of the mountain refers to nirvana and the climb is your noble path.

Right Speech

The words you speak have bigger impact on others and yourself than you think. Harsh criticism is often a gateway to anger and pain. Whereas kind words can lift the burden off even the most depressed people. Right speech means you understand what the truth is and how you can influence people and yourself for the better with your voice. Communicating effectively is one of the highest values one needs to embody. It helps in dealing with conflicts in personal and communal relationships. Harmful hate speech, useless gossips and rumors, uninvited criticism and any other communication that comes from a negative place inside you should be avoided. The goal is to communicate effectively by being mindful so that the purpose is served.

Right Action

Right Action has two components within itself - what to do and what not to do. It gives us an idea of what living in harmony can look like. We need to take an ethically sound approach to leading our life in such a way that humans, animals and the planet are enriched even after our death. Right Action comes from a sense of responsibility towards others and a feeling of inclusion and oneness. It requires that you follow the principle of ahimsa or non-violence. And it also says that you should not take anything that is not yours(stealing) or killing others or lying or intoxicating yourself with drugs/alcohol or involving in sexual misconduct. These kinds of activities are inclined to hurt others and yourself too. Thus, a Buddhist follower has to adopt the practical ethics of Right Action in daily life.

Right Livelihood

As covered in the section on "Right Action", ethical behavior that leads to harmony and peace is very important in the Buddhist tradition. This translates to your professional life as well. Right Livelihood means that you should stay away from harmful activities for your daily bread and butter. Harmful activities can be classified as those that have a strong negative impact on others' wellbeing and that lead to a disruption in the natural order. Some examples of this are drug dealing, trading in arms, selling poisons or toxic drinks, killing animals, assistance in cheating or stealing etc. Your means of livelihood is of course your choice but at the end of the day, it should not bring guilt and pain into your heart or others. Thus, Buddhism preaches ahimsa (non-violence) and opposes war or any other physical conflict.

Right Effort

Right Effort (sometimes also called right endeavor) is a virtue taught by the Buddha that encourages people to apply the right force and action against negative mental and emotional states such as anger, hatred or jealousy. The mind ought to be kept in a peaceful clear state without internal turmoil and suffering. But to do that, you need to keep these hindering negative thoughts and emotions (symbolized in Siddhartha's story as Mara and the evil army) at bay. This can be a bit tricky because the right effort entails an act of letting go of the mental baggage. This is a huge effort in itself. Often people fail to let go of that which hurts them like bad memories, bad relationships or bad attachments. Right effort means you should actively focus on clear, balanced and positive thoughts and also get rid of the evil or unwholesome thoughts. This will create a healthy environment in your mind that can nourish mindful and purposeful existence.

Right Mindfulness

For the majority of us, various thoughts and distractions of the past and the future torment us and hold us up from experiencing the present moment. We are a slave to these distractions. Nothing but the present moment is "real". Everything else is in our memory. Right Mindfulness means you should be aware of the moment and be totally focused in the present. Experiencing the present is a bit tricky. It happens so instantaneously that if you hold on to it or stay with it for too long, you will be in the past. The current moment is fleeting and to be completely immersed in it means that you let go of all the distractions and are aware of nothing but the present. However, this doesn't mean that you forget about reality. In fact, it's quite the opposite. The present moment is the only thing that's real and so, mindfulness helps us see the world for what it truly is. (We will be covering more about Mindfulness and Meditation in the subsequent chapters.)

Right Concentration

This particular component of the noble path can often be misunderstood. The original Sanskrit word for it is called "Samadhi" which refers to a state of meditative consciousness that transcends all thought and emotion. In Samadhi, there is only awareness and nothing else. It is the final fold of not only the Buddhist Noble Path but also in the Yoga Sutras of Patanjali, often considered to be the foundational text of Yogic Philosophy. Samadhi can be attained through the four stages of Dhyana or meditation. In these four stages, one is supposed to point/concentrate their meditation on certain aspects towards liberation. In the first stage, all sensual pleasures and unharmonious feelings of anger, hate, lust etc. are discarded while basic joy and happiness are maintained. In the second stage, intellectual activities are quelled and composure is retained. In the third stage, joy is also let go of but a sense of equanimity remains. And in the final fourth stage, all sensations of happiness, joy, sorrow, hate, anger, sadness are released. Nothing but pure awareness exists.

These eight elements of the noble path are sometimes grouped together into three categories – Wisdom(prajna), Ethical Conduct(sila) and Mental Discipline(samadhi).

Right understanding and right intention fall under Wisdom. These constitute the cognitive aspects of the eightfold path. According to modern science, one can say that this is the category most concerned with your analytical brain or the cerebral cortex.

Right speech, right action and right livelihood fall under Ethical Conduct. They deal with the person's relationships with external entities like other members of the society, plants, animals and the planet etc. This category is also associated with *karuna* or compassion and is one of the primary Buddhist moral values.

Right effort, right mindfulness and right concentration come under the category of mental discipline. This deal with developing your mind so as to make it "one-pointed" and focused towards total liberation. Only a mind trained in this category of discipline can hope to achieve freedom from the chaos of thought and suffering.

Thus, by adhering to this eightfold path, one can become competent in their attempt to attain inner peace, calmness and emancipation from internal conflict. In this chapter, we've covered the four noble truths shared by the Buddha and the path that can lead to the end of Dukkha or suffering.

Chapter-3: Rituals and Practices of Buddhism

Due to the practical nature of Buddhism and the way deities are looked upon, there's been an ongoing debate on whether it is, in fact, a religion. By definition, a religion has to be constituted of certain rituals and practices. Therefore, rituals are what make Buddhism a religion. It is possible to practice the Buddhist rituals and values without accepting any of the beliefs (unlike most other religions). This makes Buddhism a more secular and pragmatic religion focused on inner growth. The un-ordained practitioner (Buddhist layman/laywoman) will find it relatively easy to carry out the practices in his/her daily life.

Various rituals performed in Buddhism

Buddhism stems from the teachings of the Buddha focused towards a more wholesome life. Along with his teachings, he established a monastic and secular way of life with rules and guidelines for both paths (spiritual and material).

His teachings were very resourceful and gathered a large following. They spread across a vast region and incorporated a lot of cultural, historical and religious background from the native countries.

The different cultures that embraced Buddhism incorporated some of their rituals and practices into it. They blended the compatible customs of their own societies into Buddhism. This resulted in a religion rich with rituals and practices. Some of the fundamental rituals for all Buddhist paths are the following.

Meditation involves the practice of the mind.

Mantras are recitations of prayers and teachings.

Mudras involve hand gestures facilitating the subtle energies within.

Prayer Wheels are cylindrical wheels containing teachings or mantras.

Pilgrimage is a visit to sacred sites.

Seeking refuge means going to monasteries and focusing on one's practice.

Prayer is a seeking for blessings or fulfillment of aspirations.

Auspicious ceremonies accompany taking up Buddhist vow's or ordination, marriage, housewarming events or blessings for a new office.

Inauspicious ceremonies are related to someone passing away.

Daily rituals involve confessions, making offerings, a dedication of merit and paying homage.

In general, the dedication of merit can accompany all aforementioned rituals as it involves intent toward sharing one's blessings.

There are many facets of Buddhist meditation practice that are followed in different parts of the world to achieve different goals. In this chapter, we will look at the 3 most important aspects. Individually, they are vast enough to demand a life time of practice. But for the more beginner/intermediate learner, we will cover only the most significant concepts without much loss in the essence.

We live in a society that imposes uncertainty upon us. There are issues that our mind can't handle from an early age. This process continues into adulthood and soon our minds get too busy. A great deal of it involves the actions of the people around us which usually make us turn toward our primal instinct to protect us from discomfort and pain.

We start overthinking everything and we act out of anger, fear or try to escape our reality. Our perception of reality is sometimes distorted as a defense mechanism.

Next, we start thinking about our suffering. We may not realize it, but our suffering can't be solved by thinking. It is like sitting in your room and reading about surfing. No amount of reading can get you to feel the wave. And yet, we're not even aware of that. Getting caught up in our mind, we seek sensory pleasure and over stimulate our senses. Long term, that results in a lowering of awareness of the true nature of things around us. The obvious solution is to become more aware, or mindful.

Mindfulness

A usual misconception when it comes to the Buddhist concept of impurity of the body is that the point is to develop an aversion to sensory pleasures. Being mindful of the aforementioned is a tool to free our minds of the addiction to sensory pleasures. When you are completely mindful of your body, the sensory pleasures cease to hold you prisoner.

By practicing mindfulness, you can reach more peaceful states of existence where you get to experience joy, depend less on physical realities that are sensory illusions etc. Mindfulness is a powerful weapon that we have to add to our arsenal against suffering. But how do we do that?

The first step is to focus on breathing. Breathing is quintessential to our existence. When we shift our focus to breathing, we start to practice mindfulness. We became aware of the all the thoughts that occupy our mind.

We are being more aware of our real environment and the present moment. The next step in practicing mindfulness is letting go and to stop trying to fight those thoughts. By becoming less judgmental of ourselves and others, we decrease the power that our thoughts and emotions have over our actions.

Then we start to notice the positive aspects of reality that we wouldn't have seen if we were trapped by our undesired states of mind.

When we start cultivating mindfulness, we are easily able to distance ourselves from our thoughts. This gives us more capacity to deal with our issues. As we become more mindful of the present, our memory also improves.

With patience and mindfulness, we can come to the realization of the root cause of our problems. The practice of mindfulness can give us the energy to deal with those problems.

What comes next? When we develop our consciousness and awareness, we realize that other people are suffering too. Sometimes we might be able to help them. By shifting our focus from ourselves, our suffering which we might not be able to deal with at the present moment becomes less of a problem.

There are many ways to cultivate mindfulness. Breathing is the starting point. We can also practice mindfulness while walking. By focusing on every step and our breathing, we are essentially practicing walking meditation. For a more insightful read on mindfulness, it's immensely useful benefits, techniques and methods to practice it, you can check out my book

"Mindfulness: The Secret to Living in the Present Moment" on Amazon (link below).

www.bookstuff.in/mindfulness

For mindfulness to develop into a habit, we need to practice it daily in conjunction with a routine (preferably in the morning). With a few simple triggers and routines (explained in the book linked above), we can easily turn mindfulness into a part of our lives. At that point, mindfulness becomes a quality of our character. It becomes a way of seeing things, a way of handling and dealing with reality.

Mindfulness lets us dwell a bit deeper into our consciousness as well. We become aware of all the superficial thoughts that are on autopilot. Vipassana takes this one step further.

Vipassana Meditation

Vipassana lets us use mindfulness and the awareness of our breath to calm ourselves to a point where we get in touch with our subconscious mind.

We can compare it to an ocean. The surface of the ocean has waves that are visible. As we go deeper into the ocean, there are not many waves to notice. Eventually we can't see the currents that are present but only feel their presence.

Vipassana is a great meditation practice for beginners. There are layers to it but the basic requirement is the determination to feel more at peace within you and act in a more wholesome manner.

The first step in Vipassana meditation is to choose a position where you will feel relaxed but will still be able to focus without falling asleep.

While choosing a sitting position, the most important part is for you to feel comfortable. If you're at ease sitting cross-legged, there are a few positions you may choose – the easy pose, a half lotus or a full lotus pose.

You might want to support your back with a pillow if you experience any tension. If you're unable to sit down, you might consider sitting on a chair.

The easier pose is just sitting cross-legged;

the half lotus is placing one foot on the upper thigh of the opposing leg while the full lotus requires both feet at the opposing thighs.

Another important facet to consider is the length of your meditation session. It is advised to prepare you and ease into it. For beginners, five minutes should be enough.

You can increase your meditation sessions over time. Keep in mind that Vipassana meditation is practice, but try to make it a pleasant experience, in the sense that you're not overly exerting yourself.

If you're serious about Vipassana meditation, you can increase your sessions up to one hour in the morning and another hour at night. In longer and deeper meditative states, you might experience a significant amount of discomfort. If you do, it is advised that you consult with a meditation expert at this point. This is when your mind is doing the heavy lifting and you need someone to help you lift the burden.

Vipassana meditation is referred to as 'thought watching meditation', so it can be referred to as mindfulness meditation as well. Every movement of the body comes from the mind. While sitting still, all of the subconscious thoughts and emotions will emerge at some point.

After assuming a comfortable position, try to sit as straight as it's comfortable and lengthen your neck and spine, with your chin lightly tucked towards the neck.

If you're feeling stiffness, just experience it and try to relax those muscles. Your body remembers when it had a straight posture and with practice, you can actually improve it.

Experience the thoughts, emotions, and images as they arise and let them go. Stay as detached from them and observe them as if they're not a part of you. Continue doing this as your train of thought goes on.

There will be moments when your mind goes blank. Use those moments to rest your mind. If you observe any affinity or dislike towards a thought or a reflection, let it go. When some particularly disturbing thought patterns or images appear, simply divert your attention towards your breath.

When you experience something unpleasant during Vipassana meditation that you're unsure how to get rid of, try taking a deep breath and try to release it as you exhale.

As you clear your mind, gently bring back your attention to the body and to the breath. Observe the tranquil moment and how you're feeling during it. When you're ready, slowly lift your head up and take in your surroundings. You've just experienced a session of Vipassana meditation.

Zen Buddhism

Zen, unlike other schools of Buddhism, is focused on the process of attaining enlightenment. Unlike other Buddhist lineages, rituals and ceremonies are set aside and practice towards attaining enlightenment is the main principle.

Traditional lineages do state that everyone has Buddha-nature or the potential to be enlightened. However, that is a process that is said to last up to 10,000 lifetimes.

Zen Buddhism puts the emphasis on the practice of intuitive knowledge which is also present in other schools of thought. In Zen, intuitive knowledge is the foundation.

That notion goes to the point where all types of intellectual knowledge are questioned and only wisdom which in Buddhism is a simile to intuitive knowledge is cultivated.

There are two practices that are the foundation of Zen: Zazen and Zen Koans. Zazen is different from Vipassana in the sense that the point is to extend the periods of the blank state of mind.

In relation to Buddhism and enlightenment, it is a practice focused on emptiness or the fact that all things exist only in relation to others. Such meditation also clears the mind and promotes wakefulness.

Zen Koans are sentences that help us understand how we take our language and mental constructs for granted. They also enable Zen Masters to follow the progress of their students.

We will use two Zen Koans to try to elaborate on this. "What is the sound of one hand clapping?" This is where we can deliver some insight into Zen.

This statement would collide with common logic, as it takes two hands to clap. Most western adults would find this sentence illogical.

If you were to ask children, they are most likely to approach it in the simplest way. They will waive their hand.

That is actually the closest answer – the sound of the hand makes as it moves through the air. Zen is all about simplicity. Simple things are sometimes the hardest things to grasp as we're caught up in our world of concepts and language constructs.

Another Zen Koan state: "If you meet the Buddha, kill the Buddha."

In the literal sense of that sentence, it is in direct conflict with Buddhist teachings about compassion and even right speech. Zen Koans are not to be taken literally.

On a deeper level, this Koan means that if you meet the Buddha, you might think you've reached enlightenment. If you think you've reached enlightenment then that is not the case.

In this scenario, the Buddha is just a projection of your concept about enlightenment. Enlightenment in Buddhism is a topic onto itself, but it isn't a goal that one strives for.

The other point to keep in mind is that everything in language is contextual.

If a child starts asking about the nature of things, we will eventually arrive at an answer – "Well, that's just the way things work." If we were to inquire a scientist, we would receive a more elaborate answer based on theoretical and practical knowledge.

That is applicable knowledge which is practical in terms of technology making our lives easier by applying scientific principles. But even science is approaching a point where there is a realization that knowledge is not exact.

The only form of insight that is exact is intuitive knowledge. Zen Buddhism is about how things are related to each other, not why.

While Zen can be perceived as very rigid, it depends on the point of view. An open-minded individual that would hear Zen Masters speak might find them insightful and enjoy their creativity.

As a side note, when Zen monks start falling asleep and the teacher notices that they're straying away from practice, he might hit them gently with a stick. In Buddhism, the only certain thing being suffering, that is a very ironic solution to the issue, wouldn't you agree?

Chapter-4: Buddhism in daily life

The daily ritual starts with waking up a short while before the break of dawn, leaving time to give respect to the Buddha as a teacher to guide your journey. Early morning is convenient as there is usually peace and silence so you can focus on your actions better.

This is carried out by sitting down in a cross-legged, kneeling position or by sitting on a chair if one's physical indisposition makes them unable to keep a straight posture.

Usually, paying respect to the teacher is carried out in front of a small shrine.

A shrine is made up of a wooden stand with three levels. An image or a statue of the Buddha or a mantra written on a piece of paper is placed on the highest level.

On the next level, one can place an image of a Buddhist teacher or guardian figures, while the lowest level is reserved for offerings to the Buddha.

That can be either bowl of water or Buddhist scriptures.
If you're using bowls of water, it's important not to waste the water, i.e. re-use it for watering plants or flowers. After assuming a comfortable position, one can either practice a morning meditation, prayer or chant Buddhist lessons.

A morning meditation is very practical due to the peaceful nature of the time of the day. It can also be very beneficial as one starts the day in a calm manner which can influence how we act during the entire day. According to Tim Ferriss, best-selling author of "Tools of Titans", almost all top performers, billionaires and icons start their morning with a mindfulness routine.

The reason behind chanting is partially historical in nature as the Buddha used to start the day the same way. He chanted lessons he'd learned because chanting is action and in its nature more powerful than words.

Morning and evening prayers for loving kindness are done by reciting the Metta Sutta. A sutta is a discourse of the Buddha in Pali, while in Sanskrit is referred to by the term Sutra and means a discourse of the Buddha.

Metta means loving kindness, so this mantra is focused on loving-kindness.

Embracing the Buddhist way

Buddhism as a religion doesn't rely on faith. In fact, there are only two things that are considered dogmatic in Buddhism – karma, and rebirth. Understanding those two realities comes at a later stage in Buddhism, as lifetime of practice is considered necessary to be fully aware of how they function.

The first thing when considering becoming a Buddhist is reading up on Buddhism. You should get familiar with the basic Buddhist teachings that one could relate to, such as:

- The Four Noble Truths
- The Eightfold Path
- Impermanence
- Emptiness
- Compassion
- The Middle Way
- Buddhist practice

Upon reading those, you will encounter the fundamentals of Buddhism and some essential Buddhist terminology. Buddhism is focused on intuitive knowledge which doesn't require belief in the form of blind faith. If the fundamentals of Buddhism suit you, you are free to start practicing Buddhism as you wish.

If something seems true to you, it is likely that it will reflect in your life. Practicing

Buddhism can be a little bit daunting in the beginning especially in the western world.

There are tools that one has to utilize. Those are practice, knowledge and the middle way.

If we manage to change our behavior to be more compassionate and act in a more knowledgeable way, we can focus on the things that we can change and stop worrying about those we can't. That is what the middle way is all about.

When one decides to embrace the Buddhist way that is quite a commitment indeed. One can live in accordance with Buddhist teachings up to a point which would make one a non-practicing Buddhist.

In Buddhism, honesty is very important. So, trying to live an honest life is a good starting point. If you can't keep that up, you can live a more "easy" life (without daily practice etc.) but you should be honest about it.

The first step to becoming a Buddhist is taking refuge in the three jewels. The three jewels are represented as the Buddha, the Sangha and the Dharma.

Hey there! Just a quick check before we continue learning further. Let me ask you – How do you feel? Are you already familiar with the concepts described here? Or are you enjoying learning about these new ideas and methods? Please let me know. I want you to write a review on Amazon (link below) and be honest about it. It will take no more than 2 minutes and would mean a lot to me. Thank you ☺

bookstuff.in/buddhism-beginners-review

The Buddha means the fully enlightened one, the Sangha is the Buddhist community or anyone that has practiced what the Buddha has taught while the Dharma is the Buddha's teaching.

If we perceive the world as a constant struggle then taking refuge means seeking peace. The first step is finding inner peace. Seek and you shall receive.

Only by being in a state of inner peace, one can bring peace to others. The Buddha had said that only by bringing enlightenment towards other beings, one can truly be enlightened.

Paying homage to the three jewels is a ceremonial and symbolic initiation into Buddhism, which is done by reciting the Ti-Sarana invocation in Pali, the ancient language of the scripture.

By paying homage to the triple gem you also vow to uphold the five precepts. They include not killing any living creature, being honest, refraining from intoxicants and sexual misconduct.

In Buddhism, these are just considered guidelines however because even if you break them, it doesn't mean you can't be a Buddhist anymore. If you repent you can continue to uphold them and continue your practice.

This is best done in the presence of a Buddhist Monk but if one isn't available you can do it by yourself.

It shouldn't be done for simply ceremonial reasons but in a wholesome and willing way. The purpose of this repentance is to bring about a change in your consciousness – to make you more responsible. The chants are as follows:

Dharmam saraṇaṃ gacchāmi (x3)
[I go to the Buddha for my refuge]

Dutiyampi Buddhaṃ saraṇaṃ gacchāmi
[For the second time, I go to the Buddha for my refuge] (x3)

Tatiyampi Buddhaṃ saraṇaṃ gacchāmi
[For the third time, I go to the Buddha for my refuge] (x3)

Chapter-5: Buddhism and Science

Modern psychologists have concluded that there is a distinction between feelings and thoughts on one hand and states of consciousness on the other.

Scientists are starting to categorize these experiences while having difficulties in finding out how they relate to each other. Psychology of mind has also come to the conclusion that emotions such as anger and fear are different for every person and depend on a number of factors.

These theories are comparable to Buddhist teachings on the mind and we might even say that they're a step behind the categorization in Buddhism. Because, a Buddhist practitioner is actually utilizing what Psychology of mind is theorizing about.

His Holiness, the Dalai Lama when asked by a therapist about a unified solution to all psychological problems answered that one person's psychology is too complex to understand, let alone everyone's.

Commonalities between Buddhism and Modern Psychology

The most modern theory of mind proposes that using certain words can be dangerous, as they can lead to creating labels which can complicate issues further. In relation to Buddhism, especially Zen it's obvious that these findings correlate with the understanding of the contextual nature of words a.k.a Zen koans.

As to the relation of the mind and the nature of consciousness, psychology has turned towards MRI scanning of the brain and mapping areas where certain emotions, thoughts or mental states are visually displayed. Recent discoveries have brought light to the fact that the brain possesses the ability to self-heal and generate new brain cells. According to new studies, behavioral patterns can be changed at any age as our ability to learn new things is never completely lost.

The ability to learn new things can actually be developed by increasing the capacity of the mind to focus. What modern psychology is starting to pick up on is that this can be done by practicing mindfulness and sitting meditation – stuff Indian sages and Asian monks have been practicing for thousands of years.

Even psychiatric conditions that were thought of as irreversible can be treated with Buddhist methods. MRI imaging on expert Vipassana meditators has shown that there is exceptionally high brain activity in regions related to empathy, concentration and happiness. Also, there is reduction in brain activity at the "Amygdala" region or the reptilian brain, responsible for impulsiveness and fear.

During Vipassana meditation, one can practice having a bird's eye view of our consciousness and letting go of negative sensations. Vipassana can be a great healing process but only under proper guidance and it requires the person or patient to be an active participant. They also require a positive outlook and cultivate mindfulness up to a point where one starts to experience happiness during practice itself.

Modern science also recognizes the distinction between the observer and that which is being observed. There is the subject and the object. And they're not the same. However, according to Buddhist spirituality, there is no difference between the outside and the inside. Everything is one. This is Maya or Illusion. Logically, it is not possible to see the observer and the observed as one. However, logic is just one framework for perceiving reality. There are many ways of perceiving and interacting with reality that fall outside of immediate logic. For example, intuition is one such framework that we humans seem to be gifted with. That strong gut feeling or the deep inner hunch that things are certain way – these cannot be explained logically but are most often very real. If you're interested in exploring this, I would suggest you check out the concept of "Third Eye Awakening". As it happens, I've researched and written a book on this myself. You can get it on Amazon at the link below.

www.bookstuff.in/third-eye-awakening

The Buddhist concept of interdependence, when applied to the mind can be a bit confusing. In Buddhism, our emotional state is believed to be caused by previous experiences. Vipassana practice teaches us how to deal with those issues i.e., thoughts that result in negative behavioral patterns, and emotional states.

As a result, our experience of the present moment will improve and that will have a ripple effect on our future experiences. We cannot control external factors but we can develop methods to identify what results in harmful states of mind and either find a way to deal with it or try to avoid ones that can't be dealt with.

It's also notable that meditation has been advised as a practice by many therapists and even reputable institutions. It has already been adopted as creating sustainable therapeutic effects to counteract stress, anxiety and depression in daily life.

Psychology has extensively studied the external factors that cause imbalance in our consciousness, but Buddhism takes this one step further and offers constructive measures that can be taken to improve one's quality of life. And the empirical evidence for this is abundant in the modern world.

How Buddhism can improve your cognitive abilities

The practice of mindfulness is a process. We can start by being mindful of our breath but we should strive towards expanding it into our daily lives. When the mind is faced with a problem, it constantly works to find a solution. This can cause a lot of unnecessary suffering when the issue is beyond our capacity, be it physical or mental.

When we utilize mindfulness in our daily lives, we become a spectator to our thoughts. This calms the brain, improves focus, and enables us to function better in everyday situations. We develop a state of mind where we can easily distance ourselves from the problem which is essential to finding a solution.

Our minds work better when they're not overworked, as they have capacity available that can be utilized to focus on the issue at hand. This is a two-way street. By increasing our ability to stay mindful of the moment, we simultaneously improve our focus.

To be able to function in the modern world, we create various models of objects and phenomena we experience. This is an evolutionary trait we've picked up over millions of years. And although it has helped us progress tremendously with science and technology, it creates a fundamental gap in our interaction with reality. A complete interaction with reality, be it with action or mere observation, requires that you let go of all your mental models and cognitive biases. It may be difficult to do so at all times but nevertheless if you're seeking truth and holistic existence, it is necessary. Otherwise, our lives can be complicated to a point where we experience our daily lives as repetitive and fail to notice the ever-changing nature of being.

In order to experience happiness, we need to experience new things a.k.a novelty. However, this can lead to a constant need for sensory pleasure which can either result in forming negative habits or being unable to satisfy our endless supply of needs.

We stop seeing the beauty in the world around us as everything becomes a static construct in our mind. Life becomes routine and we can even end up feeling neurotic or anxious. Our mind needs to be happy, but we might not have the time or means to cultivate genuine happiness.

By practicing meditation (as a ritual in Buddhism), we bring our focus back to our mind. We can recognize the patterns that create these negative experiences and notice how they affect our state of mind. In Vipassana meditation, we learn how to deal with stressful situations in a safe environment.

By understanding how our mind works, we can create a conscious practice to be happy and focus on our senses without external influence. This isn't just a brain workout –

it's also devoting time to improving the way our sensory mechanisms work.

As a result, we can see our surroundings in a new   light.
In a way, we regain the natural joy that we used to experience at a younger age.

Nature is in a state of constant change and we can regain the happiness we experienced from a healthy lifestyle as we bring back the focus on our senses and experience events that we used to perceive as mundane and repetitive with new found vigor.

On the other hand, Zen meditation deals with concepts in a slightly different fashion. By deepening our understanding of the subtle realities in existence, we can free our mind from further conceptualization and make our existing surrounding interesting again. Practicing Zazen clears our mind. It also gives it time to rest and calm itself down.

When the mind is calm and resting, the senses aren't dulled by the preoccupation with daily routines and tasks. It can bring forth the healing aspect of meditation to our entire body — the nervous and the sensory systems.

And it goes both ways - by improving our overall health, we also improve our state of mind. We can then face every new day with a positive mindset and the highest capacity of our senses.

For example, we can be more mindful and experience the full pleasure of the food we eat, the beauty of nature, and pay more attention to the people around us and our environment in general. This will lead to improvement in our working environment, making it less stressful and even lead to better performance in our professional lives. It's no wonder that most of the top performing athletes, entrepreneurs and other knowledge workers leverage the power of mindful practice to experience peak productivity and results.

We should strive to expand the benefits we experience towards our personal lives as well. An undermined quality that we foster during meditation is the insight we gain which can deepen our sense of direction in our lives.

Buddhist practice accompanied by following the precept and leading the path of Dharma can create some unexpected benefits in our lives. When we become more realistic in our expectations and goals in life, we should be able to be satisfied with what we have. By simply realizing the positive aspects of our lives, our material demands will become more realistic.

What modern science & research says about Buddhism and its practices

We have already seen that modern psychotherapy has adopted meditation as a treatment. Research from Harvard has shown that during a normal work day, the mind of an average employee wanders 47% of the waking time.

Upon examining the brains of meditators, it has been observed that the areas dedicated to learning, compassion, and attention grew bigger. This is what modern science calls cortical thickening.

In layman terms, we can call this healing of our mental or psychological wounds. Ph.D. Shauna Shapiro came up with astonishing results in an attempt to scientifically prove how the practice of mindfulness affects people with problems of anxiety, PTSD (post-traumatic stress disorder) and insomnia. As one of the first scientific studies on mindfulness, the results were extremely positive.

Mindfulness was proven to improve the functioning of the immune system and normalize the negative reaction of stress hormone "cortisol". Since then, thousands of studies have confirmed these findings. Her research also showed that people who have psychological issues tend to be very judgmental on themselves. There are studies by therapists on clinical depression that have come to the same conclusion.

By being judgmental on themselves, people experienced feelings of shame, social anxiety. The physiological reaction of shame shuts down centers of growth and learning. It releases hormones that flood the system, shutting down the resources to survival pathways.

This results in a domino-effect reaction which results in even more judgment. It was derived from this that people had a tendency to hide from the parts of their brain that needed attention the most.

They somehow had the notion that this was a way to improve their wellbeing while the reality was that these parts of the mind needed to be addressed with love and attention. It was discovered that when kind attention was applied to them there were healing effects.

This is similar to loving-kindness meditation in Buddhism. Kindness boosted the ability of these parts of the brain to learn and enabled patients to change. Thus, Mindfulness became a tool that gave strength to people to face their fears and conquer them.

A starting point in this technique is embracing and spreading that energy onto the people around us, even to the people we dislike. The consequence of this practice was the brain producing happiness-inducing chemicals that restored the hormonal balance in the body.

This model of mindfulness is simple - intentionally pay attention with kindness to things that are troubling you.

When it comes to meditation, the observable results are decreased depression and anxiety along with increased pain tolerance. It has been discovered that it improves memory, self-awareness, and decision-making.

As we have seen in the previous section, meditation also has an effect on the amygdala by decreasing blood pressure and regulating the stress response. It also has a positive effect on the flow of oxygen and carbon-dioxide in the body. In yoga, this is called pranayama or controlling the life force using one's breath. Aside from improving the functions of the immune system, meditation also helps with cardiovascular disease, diabetes, and even cancer.

In a study group, where the patients practiced chanting "Om" their D.N.A. sustained less damage to bio-attacks. In western medicine, meditation has been mostly recommended for patients dealing with stress and anxiety as a complementary medicine.

The two most common forms of meditation that modern western medicine has advocated are breath-awareness meditation and chanting meditation. The first one is comprised of counting one's breath to remain focused and refrain from falling asleep.

The number of people who practice meditation in the U.S. alone has risen to 8% from one in thirty in five years. Meditation, when prescribed as a means to reduce medication, has been largely successful in the west. This should encourage further implementation of meditation into psychological and psychiatric practice.

Chanting meditation can be done by either repeating a mantra or the sound "Om". In both cases, the goal is to merge mindfulness and meditation for calming and healing purposes.

We can conclude that the more therapists have had direct contact with Buddhism or Yoga, the more competent they are at incorporating meditation into their treatment. This is usually a consequence of the degree of mental issues of their patients. Complex psychological problems such as addiction, PTSD, depression or chronic anxiety require an expert in meditation and mindfulness techniques.

Patients, or rather practitioners who want to explore different types of meditation or mindfulness practice are either referred to read up on it on their own or find a Buddhist temple or a retreat.

However, recently the medical society has brought light to the fact that meditation is a skill that requires more practice to create a more significant effect on patients. The dharma has played a major role on one of the patrons of modern Psychology, Carl Gustav Jung.

He used a wholesome method when approaching treatment, taking notice both of the mind and the spirit. He was very careful when choosing his words, recognizing the conceptual nature of one's consciousness.

Dr. David Hendricks and his wife have used this method while working with people who had problems with addiction or PTSD. The treatment had very beneficial results and culminated in a Ted talk.

Researchers at the University of Hong Kong have measured the efficiency of Buddhist practices with statistical methods. Under the guidance of Venerable Hin Hun, they have measured the influence of meditation practice on the brain and the heart.

Tests that included mindfulness practice gave the most effective results while participants were not resting i.e., when they were active. Other tests were conducted by presenting disturbing images and one test group was not chanting or chanting a random phrase whiles the other simply chanted   Amitabha.

The results confirmed that chanting has a calming effect on the heart. The most notable similarity between science and Buddhism is the method of gaining knowledge or wisdom. Buddhism relies on the perception of oneself as everyone's spiritual path is different.

This has been compared to the epistemological method by Neils Bohr, who also mentions the Buddhist view of human existence as both a spectator and an active participant in his famous model of the atom.

Nobel Prize winner Bertrand Russel stated that the scientific methods are limited when it comes to understanding abstract concepts, such as the nature of the mind and matter, what is their hierarchy, the purpose of the universe and man's positions in all of this.

He also turned to Buddhism when it came to the definition and existence of a noble life. There have been parallels between Buddhism and the theory of quantum mechanics.

J. Robert Oppenheimer compared Buddha's answer to what happens to a person after death to Heinsberg's uncertainty principle, which describes the electron's position and state.

Albert Einstein, who called Buddhism "The religion of the future", proposed a cyclic model of the universe. That is very similar to the Buddhist model which is found in the

Maha-Saccaka Sutta and Dvedhavitakka Sutta, among others.

Buddhism has had a lot of influence on modern philosophy as well. Arthur Schopenhauer's philosophical doctrine, when summarized is based on suffering (dukkha), interdependence and impermanence.

Chapter-6: Philosophy of Buddhism

In this chapter, we will look at the core philosophies that lie at the heart of the religion that is Buddhism. Over the years, through various cultural inflictions, these philosophies have diluted down to represent what the followers have found to be more practical and in tune with the contemporary understanding of reality. This dilution was inevitable since many of the original insights were either too difficult or too conflicting for the people to accept. Nevertheless, you should always keep an open mind when studying these ancient philosophies.

What is Dharma?

The Dharma refers to the Buddha's teachings. This is what the Buddha focused on during his meditations.

The Buddha's teachings were written down by his subsequent disciples.

The scriptures contain the Buddha's teachings and the intuitive knowledge that he gained during enlightenment. As such, dharma refers to "the way things are".

It should be noted that some of the teachings in the dharma weren't meant for laymen. However, those texts are widespread now and if one isn't practicing mindfulness and meditation along with learning the dharma, they can lead to misconceptions.

They are often interpreted as a pessimistic outlook on life. However, this is not the purpose of the text. With careful guidance, one can find a deeper understanding of them along with progress in the spiritual process. Learning the dharma should preferably be accompanied by practice.

The dharma covers the concepts of both material and spiritual worlds.

A very liberating teaching of the dharma is the impermanent nature of being. In context to our thoughts, it means that every state of mind is impermanent and no matter how much suffering we experience at the present moment, it's only temporary.

That holds true for pleasant experiences as well. So, to feel less suffering, we should know that they (the feelings) will not last. If we mindfully accept them in the present moment for what they are and notice how they arise and dissipate, we will not cling to them or crave them in the future.

An important teaching in Buddhism is the one about interdependent arising, or Pratītyasamutpāda. It teaches us about the nature of existence and has some overlap with concepts of Zen.

Everything exists only in relation to other things. Nothing could exist by itself. Interestingly, this applies to humans and human relations as well.

The Buddha did not dwell on the subject of the non-existence of an ego or a soul. The concept of Anatta is a complex subject and can easily be misinterpreted. It is of importance because it's a revolutionary way of thinking.

Buddhist thought is a continuation of previous eastern religions. The concept of Anatta is a novelty and there are societal implications behind its importance. The belief in a soul implicated that one is going to be reborn in relation to his/her previous existence and that there's not much one can do about it.

This was liberating for the caste system in India at the time, as Buddhism broke the chain of a belief that people are destined to be reborn as a member of the same caste.

To further expand on Anatta, the human existence is constituted of five Skandas, or aggregates. Combined, they are the entirety of one's existence.

The five aggregates are form, sensations, perception, mental activity, and consciousness. We perceive and interact with reality using these five elements.

The teaching that complements these elements of the dharma is The Twelve Nidanas. They explain the causality of human becoming and unwholesome existence.

Unwholesome actions are based on ignorance. This also means that in the Buddhist worldview, along with interdependence, judgment shouldn't be passed because it stems from ignorance, which doesn't come from an independent phenomenon. The wrongdoings cause an impermanent state of suffering because they too were a result of many interconnected phenomena that are empty of inherent existence. Any activity that comes from ignorance creates "bad" karma. Activities can create good or bad merit. This leads to either a good or a bad karmic imprint. Any karmic imprint on the world results in consciousness.

Consciousness leads to rebirth which in human form is divided into six sensory classes. The classes are eye-consciousness, ear-consciousness, nose-consciousness, tongue-consciousness, body-consciousness, intellect-consciousness.

They result in the formation of attention, perception, intention feeling and contact. The four elements are interdependent with the body.

The six sensory media arise from the six-fold sense bases.

The effect is contacting the outside world through the five sensory organs and the mind.

It is through them that we establish contact with any object in reality. The contact forms a feeling which can come in six forms. The sensation occurs when the appropriate organ comes in contact with a sensory object. A sensation reaches the mind and feelings arise.

Feeling leads to craving, and craving leads to attachment. Attachment leads to becoming which can be sensual, in form or formless. Becoming leads to birth and birth results in suffering.

Taking refuge in the three jewels requires faith. In Buddhism, faith is immersing oneself into Buddhist practice. It comes from understanding that suffering can only be transcended by practicing Buddhism and reading the dharma. An integral part is the practice of morality.

When one finds refuge in the 3 jewels, there is joy that arises naturally. By practicing meditation, reading the dharma and living a moral life, we experience blissful states, called   jhanas. As we progress in meditation, we arrive at states of tranquility. Although all of these states seem positive, meditation shouldn't be practiced with a goal in mind, as that can be a hindrance.

By keeping up our practice we experience happiness. A higher form of consciousness, called Samadhi is explained as the unification of the mind into a wholesome state of being.

Those states of mind combined result into a deeper understanding of the nature of things as they are. After one has a peaceful and focused mind, he/she can develop insight. With the right insight of the nature of things, one can start breaking the cycle of samsara.

With dispassion, or the freedom of attachment and its practice one can become dispassionate towards sensations. The craving and attachment are observed and replaced with detachment and one relinquishes the cravings that previously arose.

The next step is overcoming ignorance and impurities along with freedom from the cycle of rebirth.

Being conscious of the dissipation of the ignorance and impurities comes from reviewing the knowledge one has attained. And then, one becomes aware and certain that none of those can arise again.

What is Nirvana?

Nirvana is the cessation of suffering and overcoming the cycle of rebirth. It is preceded by understanding the laws of karma and a process of living in a fully wholesome manner, thus not generating any further karma that can result in being brought back into Samsara.

One can still be subject to the laws of karma, as was the case with the Buddha being injured during travel. The difference is that the Buddha fully embraced that as a reality that was caused by his previous karma.

In Buddhism, only human beings possess the ability to overcome their corporeal form and any other form of existence in Samsara.

However, Nirvana isn't supposed to be the goal of one's practice. It should come as a natural consequence of the devotion towards Buddhist teachings and practice.

By breaking the cycle of rebirth, one overcomes all suffering. The first step to attaining Nirvana is gaining intuitive knowledge of the dharma and freeing oneself from identifying with self, attachment to rights or rituals and skepticism along with indecisiveness. One who has broken the first three chains proceeds by gaining freedom from sensual cravings and ill-will. The Buddha himself had said that if there was one more craving as powerful as the sexual one, it would be impossible to attain enlightenment.

To become fully enlightened, one must overcome craving for the first four jhanas(states attained through meditation which are considered material existence) and the next four jhanas(states attained through meditation which are considered immaterial existence). One must also overcome conceit, restlessness, and ignorance to a full degree.

By attaining nirvana, one can become an Arahat or a Boddhisatva. An Arahat has embraced Nirvana and is freed from suffering, while a Boddhisatva has chosen the path of becoming a Buddha. A Boddhisatva can choose to return to the material world as a teacher.

This is accompanied by bodhicitta or developing great compassion towards all beings and the wish to free them from further suffering. The Buddha had said that one cannot be fully enlightened until one attempts to make sure that all other beings are freed from suffering as well.

The Buddha, when asked about nature or Nirvana explained it as a fourfold negation:

All phenomena exist: affirmation of existence, denial of non-existence

All phenomena do not exist: affirmation of existence, denial of existence

Affirmation of existence and denial of non-existence of all phenomena: affirmation of existence and denial of existence

Denial of existence and denial of non-existence of all phenomena: neither affirmation of existence nor denial of existence.

For the beginner or intermediate practitioner, it seems like a complex reality which cannot be fully explained with words.

In the latter stages of practice, Nirvana can be experienced but one might not be fully initiated to stay in that blissful state for long.

In some traditions, there is a phenomenon called instant enlightenment. When one looks inwards and notices all the thoughts, pictures or mental images she can enter a state where she realizes that she is nothing but the host of everything that arises.

If that state persists and she can attain it at will, she is considered enlightened. However, attaining such high states of consciousness doesn't come without risk. That is why Buddhist practice is usually gradual.

For comparison, higher states of awareness can be reached by using mind-expanding psychedelic drugs, but one is only an observer in the process. By practicing meditation and learning the dharma, one is an active participant.

As the Buddha was at a much higher state of consciousness than his students, there have been arguments that the messages he conveyed weren't to be taken literally but were supposed to create a ripple effect where the students would learn from the process. One can argue that the true benefit lies in the process itself.

What is Karma?

Because Buddhism is a way of life that is different for everyone, there are different explanations on what karma exactly means.

The common denominator is that it's the Buddhist explanation of cause and effect, except for the fact that it takes place in the mind. It's not linear like the cause and effect laws that are typically portrayed in science.

It's good to have in mind that Karma is a law that we can't intellectually understand and it should be intertwined with one's practice. Understanding the laws of karma comes through the long-term daily practice of mindfulness and meditation. With daily practice, we can live a more wholesome life generating better karma without intellectually dwelling on it.

Karma is the law that governs our moral actions. What we have done in the past as well as previous lives affect our present state. We are the ripening of the seeds that we have planted in the past. At the same time, the seeds that we plant in the present moment will affect us in the future.

In Buddhist practice, which is in alignment with logic, if suffering is an ingredient of our present then it had to come from somewhere. If we have lived a wholesome life but still experience negative circumstance that might be attributed to karma from past lives. We will cover rebirth as one of the fundamentals of Buddhism in subsequent sections.

Something can't come out of nothing so there must be a reason behind our struggle. The first step to deal with past karma is to repent for it. By repenting, we acknowledge harmful deeds we might've committed both in this lifetime and past ones. By acknowledging them, we can take action to diminish their effects and practice towards mitigating the effects of the mistakes we might've done.

It's important to note that karma is only one of five factors that contribute to our existence. As such, it can't be blamed for everything that is happening in our lives. That is helpful so we don't end up blaming ourselves and creating further confusion in our mind.

The five processes which constitute the order of the physical and mental realms are:

- Utu Nyama, the order by which inorganic life operates
- Bija Nyama, the way that germs and seeds develop (similar to genes in science)
- Karma Nyama, or action and result. This relates to how good deeds

generate good karma and the other way around as well.

- Dharma Nyama which constitutes an order of the higher form. Examples of this are - the physical laws of attraction and gravitation, how a Boddhisatva can become in his last birth and so forth.
- Citta Nyama is the way that mental or psychic phenomena are governed. This includes mental phenomena that are unexplained in modern science, such as telepathy or telekinesis

There is also direct and collateral karma. That is why some of the teachings of the Buddha contain advice not to associate with people that we recognize as harmful.

We create karma in the present as well. The degree to which we can influence our present actions varies from person to person. It is related to our stage of spiritual development, our mindfulness, and daily practice.

The karma we generate can be good, bad or neutral. Associating the cessation of generating further karma with a negative outlook on life can be misleading. Buddhism is a practice of getting to know the true factors that affect our happiness. If we aren't happy, to begin with, we cannot bring happiness to others. We can't even function up to par with our potential.

That is why neutral karma can have bad consequences for us. Depending on the level of our understanding of karmic laws, they can be guidelines to refrain from committing bad actions or a factor that we take into account while making a decision.

As our ignorance is the cause of undesired karma, mindfulness can strengthen our resolve while acting. Studying the dharma can result in right motivation. Those two are the basis for practice where the aim is for a wholesome state of mind where we turn what motivates us into action to the point where it becomes a part of who we are and we do it effortlessly.

Karma is the cause and Vipaka is the result. Karma can relate to the realm of the mind or the material realm. Desirable mental states are the result of good karma, just as wealth and prosperity.

The law of karma works the same way for bad karma, which results in undesirable Vipaka.

In relation to the Buddhist teachings about impermanence, there is no single entity that causes karma. As previously mentioned, the basis is our motivation which, guided by our willpower, results in our actions. The origin of karma is pure will.

There are four kinds of karma:

- Reproductive Karma which results in the sex of a person and the pain or happiness she experiences in the present lifetime
- Supportive Karma acts as an aggregate in relation to reproductive karma – if one was born with good reproductive karma it assists in health, wealth and happiness, while bad reproductive karma results in pain and sorrow
- Obstructive Karma is a way of balancing out or counteracting the reproductive karma which means that a person born unto bad reproductive

karma can experience a fruitful life and the other way around

- Destructive Karma can lead to the annihilation of reproductive karma from past lives. If the reproductive karma of oneself is developed through merit, it can limit the effect that destructive karma can have.

According to the timely nature of karma, it can also be divided into:

- Heavy karma which usually results from very good or bad deeds and usually the results manifest in this lifetime or the next
- Near-death karma is related to what one does right before death. The circumstances right before the moment of passing can lead to a desirable rebirth despite the fact that

one hasn't lived a very wholesome life. If the act of death is carried out in a self-harmful manner or the state of mind while dying has been very unwholesome while one has lived a life in line with Buddhist precepts it can lead to an undesirable rebirth.

Karma, along with rebirth, are Buddhist concepts that require belief as they can't be fully explained using logic. That doesn't mean they are dogmatic, as they can be understood through intuitive knowledge.

Is there a rebirth?

Rebirth is a concept that is considered, in many religions, to be essential to the perspective towards life and one's spiritual growth. As it's an abstract concept, it deserves to be explained so that one doesn't have to accept it as blind faith.

According to Buddhist scriptures, the stream of consciousness never stops. Just like sleep refreshes our body and gives our mind time to rest and process information, death is a normal part of the cycle of being and cessation of being.

The biggest trauma is birth which is why most of us don't recollect accounts of our previous lives.

During conception, the karma that we have created in past lives creates a unique being. If it was otherwise, life would be predetermined by our genetic predisposition.

An obvious result of the aforementioned is the fact that one's affinities or talents can be unrelated to his/her parents. We are born with skills and affinities towards art, literature or the spiritual world which are often different than what our parents had.

People are born with predispositions in life that make them act in a certain manner. That has to originate from previous life's tendencies. During his enlightenment, the Buddha recollected experience from his previous lifetimes.

Such accounts have been noted by numerous Yoga masters who had achieved such mindfulness that even the trauma of rebirth couldn't delete their memory of previous lifetimes.

Despite all that, the concept of rebirth in Buddhism is one that can't be described by a logical approach. Again, we are to follow our intuition and dwell on the concept and note if it resonates with our worldview.

Impermanence teaches us that every process, whether material or in the realm of mind is in constant change. The body experiences constant death and rebirth of the bits it's constituted of, just like our states of mind are subject to constant change.

The Buddhist cycle of birth and rebirth is called Samsara. It contains six realms. The realm of hell beings is the result of habitual killing and is comparable to hell in western religions. It differs in the fact that when the bad karma that has resulted in birth in a hell realm is exhausted, one is reborn in another realm.

The realm of hungry ghosts is a state of constant craving, while one is unable to fulfill those desires. The acts of surrendering oneself in the human realm to cravings and looking out only for one to satisfy them can result in rebirth in that realm. In the hungry ghost realm, one is driven by the same desires but constantly unable to satisfy them, which causes much suffering.

One can be reborn in the realm of animals because of a previous life where he had either killed them for food or was constantly taking advantage of them. It can also be due to attachment to the primal instincts — killing and reproduction. This is accompanied by ignoring the development of good habits and striving to benefit from others. There, one experiences constant fear for survival animals have nothing but constant fear arising from their survival instincts. After an animal dies, the karmic consequences pass towards the next realm.

And then there is the realm of demigods or Asuras. They are beings that possess greater strength and intelligence than human beings. Along with the gods, they share a celestial tree where they attempt to gain control of it against the gods. They encounter defeat and experience grave suffering as a result.

The realm of gods is reached by beings that have accumulated a magnitude of good karma. However, in Buddhism, the gods are not superior to human beings as they can't attain enlightenment. The good karma which resulted in the birth of a god and the perks that come with it slowly dissipates and one inevitably returns to another realm. The cause of the gods being unable to make spiritual progress is pride.

The human realm is the most balanced. This is in line with the Buddhist teaching of the middle way. Humans experience suffering, pleasure, and happiness but those are not as extreme as the suffering in the three realms stemming from very bad karma. They aren't as emphasized as the godly realms so that humans can have the motivation towards the dharma and practice. They are in the right state of mind to work towards improving their karma, the final stage being enlightenment.

Apart from one's way of life, rebirth is greatly influenced by the movement of one's passing from one realm to the next.

As it is obviously an important part of life. Being at peace while passing through this realm is a very positive factor. That's why, in Buddhism, suicide is interpreted as a very bad event. The mind of a person committing suicide is in great distress and the ability to be present and influence one's rebirth is very weak.

Recently there has been a debate about those realms being mental states, because everything comes from the mind. So, a person can create or interpret their reality as any of the six realms.

A point of notice is that the Buddhist concept of rebirth is different than reincarnation. There is no distinct self or soul that is being reborn, just the flux of one's consciousness transcending from one state to the next. The karmic imprint is also in constant change so we can't point to an independent construct that is being reincarnated into a body.

What is the nature of God?

Buddhism, as an organized religion, has a creationist myth. The Buddha once spoke of celestial beings that existed in a certain plane. One of them died and was reborn in the Brahmin world.

Due to the fact that the laws of time were different there than in our world, after some time, that being felt lonely.

Just as it thought of wanting a companion, another celestial being fell to the Brahmin world. That proceeded along and every next being was inferior to the beings that came before it.

The beings in that world had superior powers compared to those of humans but weren't free of the laws that govern the six realms. They were subject to karma and what resulted was the Buddhist cyclical worldview.

The Buddha rarely spoke on those matters. He focused on the human realm and things that are of more realistic value. His teachings include impermanence and the absence of inherent suffering.

Buddhist cosmology is similar to that in modern science. When Buddha spoke on the creation of the world, he also gave an overview of the destruction and the end of the world, followed by another arising.

In Buddhism, deities are beings to whom one can give offerings, as they are more in tune with some of the laws that govern our reality. Such offerings might be as showing gratitude or prayers for rain during drought.

The realm of gods is subject to the laws of karma and the laws that govern all existence. That means that there's no place for an omnipotent and eternal being in Buddhism.

In turn, the governing forces of existence are the laws of change and the karmic laws. That is why the Buddha didn't wish to comment on deities but rather spoke on how human beings can work on being free of suffering.

He focused on the matters that are more practical to human beings. The only thing that can bring us salvation is the focus on practice, morality, and knowledge.

He also spoke on the importance of being a compassionate entity, practice of loving-kindness and the importance of not being attached to earthly possessions. All these things can make humans become and act like beautiful souls.

Chapter-7: Mindfulness and Meditation

What is mindfulness?

Mindfulness is the ability to be anchored in the present moment, acting with full awareness of oneself and acceptance of the circumstances of the present moment. Practicing mindfulness can be beneficial to our ability to focus, our health, social and spiritual life.

In Buddhism, mindfulness is the seventh step in the Noble Eightfold Path. It's characterized as a means of self-control and an essential spiritual constituent.

Mindfulness is the basic practice towards freedom from suffering.

The foundation of mindfulness lies in being focused on the breath. Another form of practicing mindfulness is counting the number of breaths we take, both in and out. The final stage is being aware of the breath without breathing and the conscious focus of the mind, while still being aware of the breath. Through mastering these practices, one can progress into gaining insight into the nature of self, happiness, time and existence.

Our minds can drift off at times when we need them to focus on the task at hand. Our natural reaction can be to get frustrated which can only bring adverse side effects.

Our mind and our body are connected and only through the focus on what brings them together can we enter a state of being where the mind is at ease and in tune with the body. It's not by chance that the practice of mindfulness happens through bringing the focus back to our breath.

If we observe our breathing when we are nervous, anxious or angry – we will notice that we're breathing faster or out of rhythm. In our mind, we're not involved in any physical activity, but our state of mind affects our entire body.

A distraught mind puts too much strain on our nervous system and causes a chain reaction on all bodily functions. The same thing that can calm our body calms our mind and we can react accordingly due to a clear picture of all the sensory and intellectual factors that are at hand. In other words, we become more conscious, more awake. People often compare this experience with freedom from bondage or waking up from "the matrix".

The reality is that we might not be in tune with what's going on with our self while trying to go through our daily lives. If we live disconnected from either our body or mind and ignore the signals they're sending then after a while we will end up unable to function properly.

If we don't receive any knowledge on how to use our minds in a balanced and focused manner, we will end up with our survival instincts overwhelming us, just like a wounded animal. Luckily, there is knowledge and practice available to us and as soon as we begin practicing it in our daily lives, the better we become at taking charge of our life.

Our tasks in today's world are complex and require both physical and mental endurance and presence. While mindfulness can be a helpful practice when we're in distress or a way to improve our focus for better material results, the full benefit can only be experienced if we strive to stay mindful throughout the entire day.

This will bring more joy, happiness, and direction as well as a spiritual dimension to our lives. Some people have a hyperactive brain and can perceive it as a hindrance.

If we are able to focus a hyperactive mind on what matters to us, that will turn something we perceive as negative trait into a constructive one. This is only one of the ways that mindfulness can help transform our lives.

We might be engulfed in hurtful memories from the past and struggle to overcome them. That might reflect on our actions and our ability to learn and work with what's truly important.

When we take note of the phenomena that arise in our mind without passing judgment, we change the patterns of our thought processes. That can enable our mind to let go of the negative memories and free up space for new ones that are more positive and uplifting for the soul.

There are issues in our lives that are hard or impossible to overcome at the present moment. If we bring our attention and our focus to the ones that we can solve, the burden we're facing will pose less of a problem. You can use the technique of 'selective focus' to enhance the positive effect of good vibes and beautiful memories in your life.

At the same time, only by being mindful and remembering how we felt before can we sense the improvements. That will leave us with more energy and motivation to deal with more difficult issues in the future.

By worrying less about what's to come and using that energy to deal with the present, we will have a better experience of the present moment. However, as we are learning about letting go, we should proceed with our practice and use up all of the resources at hand. There is no such thing as being half-present. You are either fully immersed or still afloat.

To summarize, mindfulness can make us both more productive and happier. Through practicing it, we learn to appreciate the positive aspects of life and also learn how to work towards improving the negative ones.

What is meditation?

Meditation is an introspective practice where one is being aware and applying the appropriate kind of attention to mental phenomena that arise naturally. By appropriate attention we mean either letting go, being nonjudgmental or gaining insight.

Insight and understanding of mental constructs help us to overcome the more difficult issues that may arise as their root cause is ignorance. The first step is entering a deeper state of awareness and inner peace where we are in touch with our subconscious mind.

The other quality that we are developing through meditation is tranquility. In a peaceful state with no distractions, all of the capacity of our mind can be used to deal with our problems. When we are in a peaceful state, the negative emotions or mental constructs can't overwhelm us and we can start to work on overcoming them.

If the cause of suffering is a traumatic experience, we can only overcome it by cultivating kindness and acceptance. Meditation's core healing nature comes from addressing our issues with an inquisitive and peaceful mind.

When we are distracted, we can return our attention to the focal point that we have chosen. Meditation should last as long as we can stay focused without it causing unrest that we can't deal with. Our focus can either be contemplation on our breath, a simple image or a point that is in line with our sight.

True insight can be gained only with a calm mind. This state is called Samadhi and can last depending on our innate ability to meditate, our commitment and how long we have practiced. In Buddhism, inner peace and insight are connected because the right insights can be achieved only after attaining inner peace.

The posture we assume during meditation should be a sitting posture (vertical spine) at a 90 degree angle. This posture gives us the best long-term results as our energies are in perfect alignment for having an alert and active mind.

Why are mindfulness and meditation important in Buddhism?

The Buddhist teachings on living a wholesome life are more akin to guides rather than strict rules. When a person reads the dharma and comes to the conclusion that it is in line with his intuitive worldview, the ability to live in accordance with it requires that he confront his inner issues and strengthen his mind.

Through the process of meditation, a person can gain insight into his true motivation and gain a realistic outlook before making a commitment to following the Buddhist precepts. Through daily practice of mindfulness and meditation, we gain a deeper understanding of the dharma as well.

In Buddhism, there are many paths towards self-improvement and everyone has to question both his resolve and his understanding of the concepts to come up with a path where he can stay on track or progress. As one progresses in his practice, he should deepen his knowledge of the dharma with necessary further reading.

Acquiring knowledge of Buddhism is not the same as its goal – attaining wisdom and living a wholesome life. Through mindfulness and meditation, we also practice concepts that are included in the dharma. It can be said that knowledge in the dharma is helpful in mindfulness and meditation.

Buddhism has a view on intent as a precursor to action. It has a very detailed and in-depth teaching on the reasons and consequences of our actions. A lot of the Buddhist doctrines deal with the relation between actions and consequences.

When one wants to lead a wholesome life, he should be following the ethics and moral teachings of Buddhism with his whole being. There shouldn't be suppression of one's inhibitions in order to gain good karma. That doesn't help in progressing on the spiritual path.

In Buddhism, everyone is of equal importance and if one experiences suffering while adhering to the precepts, that is not regarded as beneficial.

If Buddhism isn't widespread as a religion where one resides, there can be a lot of conceptual differences between the Buddhist worldview and the modern outlook on life. That makes it difficult to have faith in Buddhism. One can compensate for that by being devoted to practice mindfulness and meditation.

As one experiences the positive changes that it has brought to the everyday life, it is easier to live in accordance with the dharma. As the saying goes, "If the student is ready then the teacher will come."

Mindfulness techniques to practice in daily life

Mindfulness can increase our quality of life when gradually introduced to our daily routine. Dedicating a few minutes of being mindful on our breath during the day can help us wind down and will contribute towards our mindfulness practice.

We can be mindful of meals bringing our full awareness which will activate our taste buds and we can fully experience the pleasure that food gives us. That can be helpful so we don't over-indulge in food in the long term.

Instead of viewing our chores, such as washing dishes, cleaning or doing laundry as a burden we can stay focused on doing everything at our own pace. It can help us not to over-exert ourselves and we can notice how well we feel when we've done a good job. The space around us has a lot of influence on our lives so keeping everything in order contributes to having more peace of mind in our lives.

When talking to other people we can pay more attention to them and create bonds with those that have a positive mindset. We can notice how they feel and try to brighten up their day. They will surely appreciate that gesture and it may reflect on their overall behavior, creating further benefits for the community.

If we feel stress or we're burdened by something, we can have a mindfulness brake. Finding a quiet spot and being aware of our breathing will bring it back to normal as our stress levels come down and we calm down as a result. This can be done in the workplace and will result in greater productivity while creating a positive mindset towards our work. You can try the popular mobile app "Headspace" for practicing guided meditation at the workplace.

When we're doing something that doesn't require a lot of effort, it's a perfect moment to practice mindfulness. Staying aware of our surroundings and noticing the small things that make us happy will add up to us having a good day and staying in a good mood.

A particularly effective tool is mindfulness while walking. Whether we're having a walk to exercise or just commuting from one place to the other, being focused on breathing and the sensations in our body while walking helps us stay energized and keeping a positive mindset.

Even though it is sometimes called walking meditation, this is essentially a mindfulness practice. Meditation is usually defined as a practice that is done while the body is still. However, being aware of our breath as we take every step can ease the mind even when it is very agitated.

How is mindfulness incorporated into Buddhist rituals?

The essence of Buddhist rituals is to be fully aware of what one is doing, why one is doing that and doing it in a skillful manner. All of the components of Buddhism are perfectly organized and are united in a way where they complement each other.

Chanting Buddhist mantras can be a way to learn a part of a teaching but the point isn't to memorize the words. When one understands what he is chanting and how it influences him or others, he will bring his whole attention to it.

The result will be a pleasant experience in itself, but there is more to it. When chanting "Om", for example, in the latter stages of one's practice the point is to do it without the sound coming from the vocal chords.

In fact, one can do it with his entire consciousness and expand the chant beyond his physical body. This is not to be understood in a magical fashion as even science has proven that the mind can have an effect on the external matter when we are very mindful or focused.

When Buddhism is practiced daily, the point of these techniques is to bring all the positive aspects and attitudes that result in action to become our second nature.

When giving offerings, for example, one should be mindful so that the act is wholesome. It shouldn't stem from one's wish to improve his life, but the lives of all sentient beings. The merit earned by that kind of offering is incomparable to one that has been done as an act dedicated to oneself. This can also be a great way to practice gratitude in one's life.

Buddhist recitations also involve mindfulness. The recitation should be done with spiritual insight, and only then it will bring everyone that is listening closely to a deeper understanding of the teachings.

When we are lighting incense or giving offerings in a temple, if we and the others around us are not being mindful of the action, we will not experience the pleasant effect. Merely doing it for the heck of it will not result in optimal experience. By maintaining mindfulness, the act will reverberate across the consciousness of all that is present and they will be the vehicle that will contribute to gaining merit.

Bringing happiness is also in alignment with the Buddhist notion that we can have an impact on our future and the future of others which is the essence of creating meaning to our existence. That holds true to bowing and prayer as well.

When performing those acts, we should be calm and bring all our focus to performing them with all sincerity. If we don't do our best to do it mindfully, we are not being respectful of something we regard as a higher power. When the higher power is not looked upon with respect then it translates to the fact that we have even less respect for ourselves and others.

Chapter-8: History of Buddhism

We have, so far, learned the various rituals and philosophies of Buddhism. We have also learned about the practices in Buddhism that make it very scientific, easy to follow and also beneficial. In this chapter, we will take a step back and look at how Buddhism actually evolved through the ages so that we can better appreciate the value it offers in the present.

Spread of Buddhism in India

After Buddha's enlightenment, he traveled along the Ganges River for the remaining 40 years of his life. His teaching drew a lot of attention because of the simplicity and the fact that a lot of people could relate to it.

This was due to the fact that Hinduism, as taught by the Brahmins made the caste system a part of the religion and a person from a lower caste was sentenced to servitude for his/her entire life.

The other religion that was prevalent at the time, Jainism, had developed many ceremonial aspects and a lot of the focus was put on rituals rather than teachings.

During the forty years of Buddha's travels, he established many monasteries and drew thousands of followers. He advised the monks to teach Buddhism in their native language.

The Buddha also established an order of nuns. Three councils were held after his

Parinirvana, with the first one taking place just after the event.

The second council saw a division between The Elders(Sthavira) and The Great Sangha(Mahasamghika). The Sthavira resulted in the creation of early influential Buddhist schools, such as the Sarvastivada, the Pudgalavada, the Dharmaguptakas and the Vibhajyavada.

Vibhajyavada is noted as the precursor of Theravada Buddhism. Mahasamghika created a Transcendentalist school of thought, which is considered the precursor of Mahayana Buddhism.

The issues arose over the rules for the monastic order between the Elders and The Great Sangha. The third council also witnessed the creation of the Abhidharma. The Abhidharma was the first systematic teaching which sought to unite the suttas into a school of thought that explained all phenomena of existence.

The suttas were what the Buddha's followers had written down from his discourses. A figure that contributed to Buddhism spreading further was king Ashoka. As the founder of the Mauritian Empire, he reigned for eight years before waging war with the Kalinga Empire.

The battles and destruction he saw caused great remorse and he sought to reform his kingdom into a peaceful one. King Ashoka embraced Buddhism to the point that he created social and political norms where Buddhism could flourish. During his reign, monks even had a degree of influence on political decision making.

After Ashoka's death, the downfall of the Mauryan empire was attributed to the focus on building a peaceful society. A military coup of sorts placed a commander-in-chief as the leader of the country and a period of stagnation took place.

There is questionable evidence for Buddhist stupas being destroyed and 100 gold coins were offered for the head of every monk. Monks migrated to the southeast and found refuge in the areas of Gandara and Mathura around Amaravati (current capital of the state of Andhra in south India).

During the invasion by the Yuezhi nomads in the 1st century B.C.E., the Kushan Empire was established in northern India. Gandharan Buddhism saw its peak and many Buddhist temples were built or renovated.

Emperor Kanishka was particularly keen on Buddhism and contributed both to the spread of Buddhism to south-east Asia as well as compiling extensive commentaries on the Abhidharma. He sought help from 500 monks to contribute to compiling the Abhidharma verses and commentaries.

It is said that three hundred thousand verses and over nine million statements were compiled over a period of twelve years. During the Hephalite reign of the Gandara region, Buddhism continued to thrive. After their downfall, it still kept its tradition in certain areas of the country.

Buddhism in China, Tibet and Southeast Asia

Buddhism entered China at the beginning of the 2nd century A.D. through the Silk Route. Despite many critiques and a rough start, its presence grew in a matter of decades.

With the fall of the Han dynasty, the dominant Confucian ideology was questioned amidst political turmoil and the Buddhist influence grew. This was partially due to rulers who weren't of Chinese background trying to gain power. Through China, Buddhism spread to Korea and eventually to Tibet.

Even though Tibet had contact with monks at an earlier period, Buddhism made heavy impact in the middle of the 6th century A.D.

Tibet received monks from both Indian and Chinese lineage and a conflict emerged between them. The Chinese lineage was disbanded after a debate in favor of the Indian one.

King Ashoka's son, who was an ordained monk, took to Sri Lanka. He converted the ruler of Sri Lanka and established a bond between Buddhism and the kingship which lasted for two centuries.

The next destination for Buddhism was Burma. There, Buddhism coexisted with Brahmanism and various local cults. By the 2nd century A.D., Buddhist monks had spread the teachings of the Buddha throughout Thailand, Cambodia, Vietnam, and Laos. By the 5th century A.D., Buddhism reached Indonesia and the Malay Peninsula. While Buddhism spread throughout Asia,

Hinduism gradually emerged as the dominant religion in India.

With the expansion of Islam, its influence was further diminished. The Buddha was assimilated into Hindu religion in the sense that he was represented as a god, or one of Vishnu's incarnations.

Spread of Buddhism to the west

There have been a few accounts of Buddhism reaching the west during medieval times. In the modern period, before westerners expressed an interest in Buddhism, many migrants from China and Japan came to the west, followed by large groups from Southeast Asia. They kept their religion and some of their descendants played a vital role in building a presence of Buddhism in the west.

The late 19th century saw renowned theosophists Henry Olcot and Elena Blavatsky convert to Buddhism. After the first conversions from the west, a few others followed suit.

Along with immigrant families, a few monks migrated to America. In 1899, they established the Buddhist Mission of North America. A delegation from Japan represented Buddhism at the World Parliament of Religions in Chicago not long after.

D.T. Suzuki had been the most prominent figure to promote Zen Buddhism at that time in the West. His work with Paul Carrus merged western transcendentalism along with Buddhism, creating a school of thought that came to be known as Buddhist Modernism.

The first Buddhist temple in Europe emerged in 1924 in Berlin. It was an initiative by Paul Dahlke, who had studied Buddhism in Sri Lanka before the First World War. Three years later, two books were published on Buddhism which drew attention to it. The Tibetan Book of the Dead "Bardo Thodol" and Alexandra David-Neels's "My Journey to Lhasa" mostly popularized Tibetan Buddhism.

The early interest of the west in Buddhism was hampered by poor translation. Western intellectuals soon took to learning Asian languages.

The precursor to a widespread western Buddhist movement was Jack Kerouac, as the book "The Dharma Bums" found a wide audience. A mix between New Age philosophy and eastern philosophy, in general, can be found in Alan Watts's books as well as many talks on Zen Buddhism and Buddhism in general. His talks are still popular among beginners showing interest in Buddhism.

Shunryu Suzuki's arrival to America broke the ice when it came to renowned Buddhist teachers visiting the country. His presence alone inspired enthusiasts. Philip Kapleu, who was one of the few westerners taught by ordained Zen Buddhism monks, wrote a book on Buddhism titled "The Three Pillars of Zen". With permission from his teacher, he formed The Rochester Zen Center in New York in 1965.

The same year saw the opening of the Washington Buddhist Vihara by a group of monks from Sri Lanka. It was the first establishment from a Theravada lineage which taught Vipassana meditation. The Vipassana movement saw greater interest after a group of Americans returned a few years later. They had studied Vipassana meditation from masters in Asia.

The 1970's saw the largest growth of interest in Buddhism in the west. The cause of attention was compassion towards Buddhists being persecuted by the Chinese government, but Americans also discovered about the abundant Buddhist culture in Tibet.

Many Tibetan Lamas opened Buddhist centers in the States. All of the main Buddhist schools of thought became widely known. Thich Nhat Hanh founded a Buddhist retreat center in France and his extensive written work sparked interest towards Engaged Buddhism and Vietnamese Zen.

With the present Dalai Lama's first visit to the United States, his composure and direct approach made him a well-known public figure. As a spiritual leader of the Tibetan people who were well versed in English, his media appearances inspired movies along with a following from American celebrities.

A number of American soldiers who remained in Asia after the Korean and Vietnamese wars sought refuge in Buddhism and were ordained as Buddhist monks.

Buddhism is practiced in western countries today on a large scale. Apart from The United States and Europe, Buddhism in Australia witnessed a large increase in following as well. Australia has adopted eastern religions and medicine and incorporated it into official institutions.

A notable Buddhist group in the west is *The Foundation for Preservation of the Mahayana Tradition.* Its constituents are available in 142 teaching centers across 32 countries.

Western Buddhism has also conceived Buddhist Modernism. The most notable are the Shambala Meditation Movement, the Triratna Buddhist Community, and The Diamond Way organization. Ole Nyadhl, the head of The Diamond Way organization has founded over 600 Buddhist communities.

Chapter-9: Present day Buddhism

In this chapter, we will learn how Buddhism has changed over the years and what significance it holds for the present-day followers.

Buddhism is essentially a way of life more than anything else. As the Buddha had said, the path to enlightenment is different for everyone. With the spread of Buddhism over the years, it has encountered change due to internal and external factors.

Internally, it has changed as upon studying the scriptures, monks and teachers have come up with new techniques and systematization of Buddhist practice. Externally, Buddhism has adapted to the cultural situation in various countries.

The fundamentals of Buddhism haven't changed over the years however there have been subtle modifications to their interpretations. Among Westerners, there have been devotees to Buddhism which have strived to learn Buddhism towards becoming ordained Buddhists while others have focused on the practical applications.

The earliest account of a Buddhist school, Theravada Buddhism is still prosperous in Sri Lanka and Vietnam. It is the closest form of original Buddhist practice with a distinct separation between monks and laymen. It is constituted of studying the original texts as well as the begging tradition of monks and meditation.

Upon reaching Tibet, Buddhism faced a culture that had a lineage of deities and myths. The Tibetans embraced Buddhism, but it was intertwined with the local culture. Therefore, the Tibetan Buddhists fused the present rituals, along with the strict monastic ways. They added a hierarchy in terms of Buddhist education and the order of the monks.

In the 11th century, a textual account called Lamrim, representing the stages of the path was introduced. They are versions of an elaboration gave by Atisha called "A lamp to the path of enlightenment".

The text divides every person according to their attitude in this life and what they are to practice:

- A lesser person should dwell on the positive sides of birth and contemplate impermanence and death
- The middle person should focus on the laws of karma, suffering as well as the benefits of liberation from suffering and transformation
- The superior humans are constituted of the four Brahmaviras, the boddhisatva vow, the six paramitas and tantric practices.

The purpose of these texts is to guide the practitioner on his spiritual path in a logical order.

A tantric view is a form of Vajrayana adopted in Tibet. It focuses on visualization techniques to meditate on which in turn bring one to release suffering faster. The concept behind this is, as humans are subject to attachment, it is through focusing on dissipation of this attachment that they can attain enlightenment.

The spread of Tibetan Buddhism to the west caused implications and effects on the state of Buddhism in the east. Different Buddhist schools of thought are starting to collaborate and exchange ideas and practices.

In Tibetan Buddhism, venerated lamas that preserved the teachings usually gave precedence to monks with higher stature in the past. But they are starting to speak out to a wider audience that includes beginner practitioners. There is an effort to overcome some of the gender issues in Buddhism as well. Stemming from western nuns, who received full ordination from other traditions caused an order of fully ordained nuns.

The efforts of the Dalai Lama have contributed a great deal to the Western science of the mind. This has brought progress to Tibet. For example, translation of written material enables monks in the east to learn the basics of western science.

By spreading Buddhism to the west, Tibetan culture has benefitted in breaking its dogmatic worldview. Buddhism as a religion is still being preserved in its original form.

When Buddhism reached China and Japan, it encountered a simpler approach to life. With the Japanese roots of Zen Buddhism, the original religion was reconfigured.

In relation to attaining enlightenment, two schools of thought emerged. The focus was on drastically changing the mental state of the practitioner by introducing Zen Koans and long meditational practices.

In Sri Lanka, the minor Theravada traditions received patronage from the community. After the 12th century, however, these traditions were abolished.

Along with keeping major Buddhist schools from the Theravada traditions, some Mahayana practices were introduced. Recitation of Mantras and counting prayer beads had been observed among Mahayana monks.

India has been subject to the caste system and Buddhism by default is an excerpt from their implication. It is no wonder the Dalit (untouchable) caste which has distanced them from the system has embraced Buddhism. A political activist of the Dalit caste, Dr. B.R. Ambedkar has reintroduced the idea to Indian society while merging political ideas with Buddhism.

In his book "The Buddha and his Dharma", he merged Marxist political ideas and proposed that Buddhism along with political activity can bring equality in social terms. In his view, this would lead to less suffering. Buddhism has often stayed away from messing with social issues, but there have been accounts that are exclusions to the rule.

Perhaps more important to the general idea of changes is Buddhism is the birth of the Vipassana movement. It is a modern take on Buddhist practice, while the Vipassana Research Institute has taken the role of the most influential organization. Vipassana has also been promoted as a practice among non-Buddhists and the organization has offered classes to companies and institutions.

Buddhism in Japan, due to the society and culture being technologically oriented, has become subject to scientific studies. The outside view on Japan as a preferred destination may not hold true.

The Japanese society may benefit a lot by implementing Buddhist practice and ethics. It is common knowledge how the Japanese are overworked and that societal norms are very strict because the ordinary man has become similar to people in the west. Introducing Buddhism to science gives hope that it can be an entry point into a wider audience.

China, under the reign of Emperor Xuanzong, saw the arrival of the Kaiuyan's three masters. In the Daxing Shansi temple, they established a form of esoteric Buddhism. Translations from Sanskrit to Chinese were made that were supported by the court.

They brought an esoteric, dynamic and magical teaching that encompassed the material world along with the spiritual. It included a detailed mantra formula and rituals to protect a person or a kingdom, affect a person after death and bring rain during a drought.

The last miracle was the main reason they were received by the emperor and treated with great respect. Their teachings reached a point where the emperor ordered the upper class to favor them instead of Daoism.

Even though they fell out of favor during the ruling of the next emperor which led to the persecution of Buddhism, the teachings still survived and were transmitted through a secret lineage of monks. They even reached Japan in the form of the esoteric school of Shingon.

From the original teachings of the Buddha and the different interpretations of latter teachers, four major schools of thought in Buddhism prevailed. In Buddhist nomenclature, these are considered lineages. Contributions to these teachings have been attained through practice, personal experience and interpretation of the Dharma.

There are four Buddhist lineages practiced at present:

- Theravada
- Mahayana
- Zen

- Vajrayana

Vajrayana is considered as a part of Buddhist practice (and not a lineage in particular) in some Buddhist schools.

Theravada

Theravada is a Buddhist lineage that has the biggest similarity to historical Buddhism. It is written in the ancient Pali Canon and is regarded as a conservative form of Buddhism. It draws its origins from Sri Lanka but has spread across Southeast Asia. It's also the lineage that most Buddhist emigrants uphold.

The characteristics of Theravada are that knowledge comes first, followed by practice and cessation of suffering. It has strict rules for monks and this caused the various internal divisions that occurred in the past.

In Theravada, the attitude towards insight is that it comes instantly. That is similar to the Vipassana movement and sounds similar to Zen Buddhism. Theravada contains the most extensive written knowledge of Buddhism.

Even though it's considered conservative, it is regarded as the source of modernist Buddhist traditions. The reason may lay in the fact that most people that come into contact with Buddhism often meet Theravada first and the main concepts are very close to the original teachings of the Buddha.

The second lineage, Mahayana Buddhism, has the widest following of practitioners around the world. The term originates from

Boddhisatvayana or the Buddha as a vehicle for enlightenment.

Mahayana

In Mahayana, the notion is that one's personal spiritual path is not enough for achieving full enlightenment. Thus, the focus should be on benefits for all sentient beings. Monks are encouraged to prioritize sharing their insight and lay practitioners should meditate towards developing a state of mind in which they distance themselves from the notion of self.

In Mahayana, the Buddha is seen as a deity of sorts who consists of three parts. Meditation is practiced by visualizing the Buddha, seeing oneself as the Buddha or repeating the name of the Buddha.

The teachings of Mahayana consist of texts that can have different interpretations which can all be true at the same time. The goal of Mahayana is attaining bodhicitta and Buddha-hood as soon as possible. This is due to the fact that an enlightened being benefits other beings the most.

Vajrayana

Vajrayana, the fourth lineage, is sometimes considered a part of Mahayana. Some of the derivatives from Mahayana are Madhyamaka, Yoga-Cara, Buddha Nature and Buddhist Logic which is the latest. Buddhist logic is a western scientific analysis of the reasoning that Buddha used, which seems transcendental and accurate to this day.

Chanting Mantras and being mindful of the Buddha is an integral part of Mahayana practice. The term "Great Vehicle" expresses the way that the Buddha taught the dharma. It represents a sort of historical outlook of the dharma as it has evolved through the years. This is not only true for the dharma itself, but for the clarity and the way it was understood while having in mind that it was a progressive process.

Vajrayana is sometimes called esoteric Buddhism. Along with Mantrayana, Tantrayana, Tantric Buddhism and Esoteric Buddhism, they create a system of practices for the faster attainment of enlightenment and freedom from suffering.

Vajrayana is also known as the "Thunderbolt vehicle", referring to a mythical weapon. This is a metaphor for tantric practices in Vajrayana.

Vajrayanists gathered a large number of Tantras which have evolved into a method of Buddhist visualization practice. These were initially used in rituals that don't conform to Buddhism but were incorporated and transformed at a later stage and incorporated into Vajrayana practice.

In Vajrayana, the mundane samsara world coexists with sacred nirvana in a continuum. There have been other Buddhist schools of thought that have upheld this belief.

The perfection of insight in Vajrayana is often compared to that of Mahayana Buddhism, but Vajrayana teachers argue that their practice works faster. As Vajrayana draws its roots from the teachings of a wandering group of Yogi's, many of its practices and teachings seem like a cross between Yoga and Buddhism.

The goal of Vajrayana practice is similar to that of Mahayana. The path differs and is constituted of focusing on Buddha-nature. This is to enable the innate Buddha nature of human beings to identify with their Buddha nature and attain enlightenment.

There is a form of a sacred bond between the teacher and the student in Vajrayana, while the student forgoes transformation. The dialogues between them can be harmful if an outsider listens to them so they are kept secret from the outside world.

A specific practice in Vajrayana is overcoming the duality of nature. Impure and defamatory substances of bodily origin are accepted and used in rituals, sometimes as offerings to overcome the dual view of the mind.

Tantric practices which involve sex are not meant to bring sensual pleasure but rather bring one closer to the object of worship, which is Buddhahood. Emphasis is put on the female aspect of nature and humans as the element of worship for the sake of nurturing love.

What modern Buddhists practice and follow

In the modern world, Buddhist practice varies among different cultures and countries. In countries that have a history of Buddhism, practice, and following of the teachings generally depends on the Buddhist lineage.

In western countries among Buddhist emigrants, the practice and following are usually inherited. People of western origin have adopted Buddhist practices rather than following lineages. Although there are some who have sought a spiritual path in becoming Buddhists and even some who have been ordained, the fact is that most of the westerners practice what seems practical to them.

Another form of Buddhist practice is the meditation that has been developed by experienced traditional Buddhists for therapeutic purposes. That type of meditation is meant for healing but it can also be practiced for cultivating qualities that are developed through standard

Buddhist practice and knowledge of the dharma.

It's important to note the distinction between modern Buddhism and Buddhist modernism. Buddhism, in general, has had many sectarian movements but few have active participants as to this day.

Among westerners, the type of practice followed usually differs from one's circumstances, motivations, and location. If there is an active Buddhist society near the home of the practitioner it is much easier to fully embrace the Buddhist way.

This is because Buddhism is a path that is very different than one's upbringing and one would need guidance as it would be complicated to incorporate it in daily life. One would need a lot of courage and determination to follow it independently as the western society and norms are culturally very different from what one needs to take refuge in the three jewels.

What is more common among westerners is starting the practice due to some events in one's life. Whether it's a mental or a physical ailment, it's not unusual for an agnostic person to find Buddhism much closer to his natural beliefs than religions that have an omniscient deity as the focal point of worship.

When one gets in touch with Buddhism in the western world and considers Buddhist practice, it's usually due to seeking something more out of life or a solution to a problem. It is very beneficial to have guidance either from an active Buddhist community or a monastery.

While there are Buddhist centers across the world, Australia has the most active and diverse presence of Buddhism among western countries. There are dharma talks and monks available for consultation on what to practice to change one's mindset to become more positive.

In the United States and Europe, Buddhist practice has become a part of psychology and psychiatric therapy. Modern therapists usually recommend the breath-counting mindfulness technique as a starting point because their patients haven't attained enough control over their mind and being.

If the patient responds well to this type of practice or needs to apply more effort to have appropriate results, the method of choice is Vipassana meditation. Vipassana is known to bring a calm state where one can overcome tougher mental hardship. In the case of Vipassana meditation, the therapist needs to have the appropriate skills and understanding to guide their patient through the whole meditation process.

The lifestyle in the west is often stressful and the scientific community is becoming aware that medicine only treats the symptoms of the consequences of daily stress. There are only so many pills that can be prescribed to someone who is, at a fundamental level, unable to handle the utter emptiness of reality.

When a person starts to practice mindfulness and meditation, she doesn't have to adopt Buddhist beliefs. This is not detrimental in itself as the practitioner that has sought refuge in the practices doesn't have to focus on her spiritual development necessarily.

When a western practitioner usually starts practicing mindfulness and meditation, the benefits she receives generally depend on the motivation, perseverance and how well she's been informed. Such practitioners usually don't uphold the five precepts before a certain stage as their mental state is too much off-balance.

It's not unusual for someone who has benefitted from the practice of mindfulness and meditation to gain further interest in Buddhism and the dharma. That interest usually results in being more informed, or developing an intellectual understanding of what one's practice is actually based on.

An aspect that is hard to overcome among westerners, in general, is connected with sexual misconduct and right speech. The first part is due to the nature of the attachment to sex and the second one is mostly a societal norm that one has grown used to. This is nothing to be judged on or turn our eyes away from. We have to approach it from an honest place with nothing but curiosity and love.

The difficulty of upholding the Buddhist precepts usually depends on one's upbringing, social status, and education. They also depend on one's determination and innate talent as they would require a high degree of mindfulness. Language is deeply rooted in our brains and changing speech patterns can be quite difficult, especially if one stays amongst her peers.

It is unfortunate that it may depend on the status of the individual, as being an ethical person has become a challenging task these days. The obligations towards one's family or even one's own material existence can make it difficult to incorporate Buddhism in one's daily life.

Buddhist practice can become a powerful tool for an individual in self-improvement. When that practice is detached from the core teachings then upholding them can turn that tool against the society the person is a part of.

In the case that the practitioner is a selfish individual, his individual capacities can grow. That is one of the aspects that the Buddhist community has noticed as misuse of skillful means. The reason that Buddhist texts were kept as esoteric teachings is the practice just for the sake of acquiring a competitive edge.

As we can find information about almost anything through modern media, Buddhist teachers are inclined to offer their service to keep Buddhist practices and beliefs to remain constructive for the general public.

Today, there are many therapists and psychiatry professionals that have dealt with difficult issues and people with a state of mind that western medicine doesn't have tools to repair. Among such professionals, a deeper interest in the practices and philosophy of Buddhism comes naturally. They might take it a step further and decide to visit a monastery so they can give better instructions to their patients.

Individuals that benefitted from Buddhism and overcame difficulties like addiction, depression or anxiety can be very persistent in their practice. It is said that without experiencing difficulty, spiritual progress is hard to attain.

People who are not part of a close family or community and have come into contact with Buddhism, upon deciding to follow the path usually seek a monastery where they can focus on their practice in an environment that isn't obstructive to their personal growth and fulfillment.

There have been numerous accounts where westerners seek work in farms in Sri Lanka just to be able to listen to Buddhist teachings and focus on one's practice. Depending on their resolve they can join a monastery and if their motivation is strong enough they may continue to stay there.

The ideas that one has about Buddhist monastic life might not be in line with reality, as becoming a Buddhist monk is not an easy task. If that was just a phase in one's life, such practitioners won't be able to deal with the dynamics of the life of a Buddhist monk.

There are ordained westerners who have created monasteries or helped in establishing them under the guidance of their teacher. They usually hold dharma talks which relate to western mundane life as well as challenging issues, such as ailments.

The cultural and language barriers are hard to overcome and if those students haven't learned from the original texts or haven't spent enough time to develop the skill of becoming a teacher, that Sangha (community) might be a compromise between western lifestyle and the original Buddhist teachings.

Can we practice Buddhism as a secularist?

Buddhist practice doesn't involve idolatry. Buddhism is also respectful and compassionate towards different cultures, religion, and worldviews so the teachings can resonate with secularists.

Most of what the Buddha has taught as well as the practice of meditation and mindfulness is very beneficial to one's quality of life, especially if they want to uphold certain moral and ethical standards.

As such, secular Buddhism has actually developed as a movement. The roots can be traced back to Japanese Zen and Korean Seon Buddhists schools and during the Renaissance period where secularism was reintroduced through the teachings of Greek philosophy.

By interpreting the teachings of the Buddha in accordance with the worldview of a secularist, some of the teachings that have to do with tradition and the ceremonial aspects are being relativized, while those that are inclined towards one's psychological and ethical aspects are being upheld.

The notions that involve something that can't be epistemologically perceived are being disregarded. While taking into account the historical and cultural aspects of the time and place the Buddha lived in, there are texts that don't resonate with secular Buddhists.

That holds true for the attributes that are given to gods or Boddhisatvas and Buddhist cosmology. There are some ethical views, such as the passing of merit through karma and abortion where secular Buddhists differ with original teachings. However, the original rules should be interpreted as mere guidelines. The Buddhist way is not to setup hard and fast rules and limit the expansion of our soul.

Secular Buddhism is focused on finding the meaning of the teachings of the Buddha in relation to the cultural context which would imply that the original texts have a different meaning now because the circumstances have changed.

That doesn't negate that the Buddha was right. It only means that the way he was understood at the time isn't how secularist Buddhists interpret his teachings now. The Buddhist concept of rebirth is also being disbanded in favor of the benefits of more pragmatic Buddhists practices towards enlightenment in the present lifetime.

Secular Buddhism also questions the authoritarian structures and progression during meditation, which is encouraged to be a matter of strictly personal insight in this form of Buddhism.

There is a widespread secular Buddhist movement throughout the west. A famous teacher of Vipassana meditation once taught this to a secular Buddhist and said along the lines that it is "something everyone can benefit from: the art of living".

There is also the account of an ex Theravadin monk, Jack Cornfield in an attempt to spread the benefits of Buddhist practice, presenting Buddhist meditation without the ceremonial and cultural aspects. These approaches can be formulated as applied philosophy, rather than a religion.

Chapter-10: Common myths and misconceptions

Myth #1: Buddhism is not a religion

The practical nature of Buddhism and the lack of worship of deities had lead people in the past to believe that Buddhism is not a religion. By definition, every organized form of spiritual practice with a monastic order, rituals and ceremonies is a religion.

Although Buddhists do not believe in an omnipotent being, it could be argued that every enlightened Buddhist teacher is omniscient – in Buddhist terms. Even though the emphasis in Buddhism isn't on dogma, there are two dogmas that everyone who declares themselves Buddhist accepts.

Those are karma and rebirth. So, the emphasis is not so much on the dogmatic part itself as it is on their value in connection to the other teachings.

Buddhism doesn't focus on worshipping deities but it also doesn't renounce them. There is a place for them in Samsara, the Buddhist circle of life but they aren't considered superior to all humans. Buddhist practice isn't focused on becoming a deity or demi god but rather an enlightened being free from suffering.

Myth #2: Buddhists have to be vegetarian

In accordance with the Buddhist precepts for monks or lay people, if one hasn't willfully killed or directly contributed to killing a being, it's not considered to be against the precepts. Buddhism doesn't put too much emphasis on what one eats.

It rather deals with overindulgence of food. In simpler societies, monks used to spread the dharma and helped ordinary or lay people with mundane issues by begging for food. After a monk was accepted in a home, he was offered food as a kind gesture.

The monk used that occasion to talk to his hosts and without imposing Buddhist beliefs on them, he tried to guide them through their hardships. Buddhists are encouraged not to be picky about their food as that attention is best used in practice.

Myth #3: Buddhism has a nihilistic view of life

Buddhism has recognized the obvious fact that there is much suffering in the world. In its worldview, a lot of that suffering can be avoided. This process involves education, upholding certain values and enough practice.

Buddhism is an active religion which enables its followers by giving them the resources and guidance to help themselves. Suffering is impermanent and the duration of every undesirable state of being should serve as motivation to overcome it.

One should practice and work towards cultivating circumstances for living a happier, more fulfilling life. Buddhism doesn't focus on promoting the fact that the human condition is undesirable by default but rather towards inner change. Inner change only comes through faith in overcoming difficulties and belief in one's ability to stop creating further hardship for oneself and for others.

According to Buddhism, there is always hope but hope is not enough. Willful action and commitment to the wellbeing of all is the "Middle Way" that Buddhism advocates.

Myth #4: About Buddhism and Reincarnation

This fallacy comes mostly from misinformation and the idea that all eastern religions are alike. To be more specific, reincarnation is the term most often heard about in Hinduism. There is an essential difference between Buddhists who believe in rebirth and religions that accept the phenomenon of reincarnation.

The Buddhist teaching on impermanence and no inherent existence means that nothing exists by itself and nothing has permanent nature. Thus, there is no possibility of an eternal soul.

The karma that we generate is also subject to constant change. During rebirth karma isn't the only factor that comes into play. It is the law that governs the moral and ethical actions.

<u>Conclusion</u>

One thing that we can derive from the spread of Buddhism worldwide is that modern science can't completely tackle the issues of the mind and the inner dimension. The fact is that science is seen as progression and it's hard to accept the idea that teachings that have existed for millennia need to be studied and applied under proper guidance.

A global society focused on materialism and science has made it hard for the individual to find his/her place and attain inner peace. Materialism shouldn't be understood in a negative way as people need food, clothes, and technology to survive.

The global and local organizations that are meant to deal with issues that people can't haven't offered a solution to problems and have focused on the symptoms rather than the source of the disease.

Buddhism is formulated in a way that doctors at the time used to diagnose and treat patients. It is that kind of reasoning which is applied to the mind. It doesn't deal with a mental disease but suffering in general.

That is one of the facts that have brought so much global attention to Buddhism and Buddhist practice. Currently, Buddhism in the west is seen as a tool to improve one's productivity or mental health.

While this is an important part of Buddhism, we can safely say that the teachings and practice of Buddhism aren't limited to a more convenient life for oneself. It's often said that spirituality – especially moral and ethical values haven't kept pace with science in the world.

Buddhist teachings on how to conduct oneself in order to prosper are in line with logic. One can argue that they're the most developed system of values. That is why Buddhism has embraced science too.

Present religions have been manipulated through the years and the results have created global conflict. It is not the fault of religions themselves, but the interpretations of teachings that can be misconstrued and give excuses for a large source of negativity and animosity between people.

While the west has embraced Buddhism, so far, it's focused on the personal benefits.

Maybe the fact that meditation contributes to spiritual growth can spread the popularity of the accompanying Buddhist teachings and shed the misconception of their historical deprecation.

The materialistic worldview in the west has reached its apex and is standing on thin ice. People are glorifying billionaires and film stars while ostracizing teachers and social workers. Buddhism offers firm ground for humanity to catch up with the scientific progress. We need to be aware that western Buddhist practice, as well as other contributions from the east, had been watered down over the years. It remains to be seen if the west sees value in the Four Noble Truths and the eightfold path. Nevertheless, immense value and personal treasure await anyone who is curious enough to explore and disciplined enough to practice.

That brings us to the end of this book. I would love to hear your thoughts on what you learned and how you felt during the read. You can leave a review on Amazon by going to the link below and sharing your honest opinion. It'll help me a lot with my own journey of serving you and other readers as well. Once again, I thank you from the bottom of my heart for getting this book and giving it your valuable attention.

bookstuff.in/buddhism-beginners-review

More books from Dharma Hazari

Mindfulness: How to Live in the Present Moment (Practical tips and Daily Routines)

Chakra Healing: How to Unblock and Awaken your Chakras

Empath: How to deal with emotional sensitivity and Begin healing your energy

Made in the USA
Middletown, DE
31 January 2023

23595040R00132